W9-CQB-959

MEDITERRANEAN

SEA

LEBANON

Tibnîn
HULA VALLEY
Al Qunaytirah
As Sanamayn

Nahariya

SYRIA

Acre
Mt. Meron 3962
Safad
Capernaum
Lake Kinneret (Sea of Galilee) -696
Ein Gev

Carmiel

Haifa
Mt. Carmel
Ein Hod
Nazareth
Tiberias
Mt. Tabor
Gader (Ruins)
Dar'a

JEZREEL VALLEY

Caesarea
Afula
Megiddo
Beisan
Irbid
Al Mafraq

Hadera
Janin

Nathanya
Tûl Karm
Shomron
Jarash

Az Zarqâ'

Herzliya
Nablus
Zarqâ'

Yarkon
Petah Tikva
As Salt
'Amman

Ramat Gan
Tel Aviv-Jaffa

Rishon le Zion

Ramla
Lod
Arîha

Rehovoth
Jericho

Ashdod
Latrun
Jerusalem
Ma'daba

Ein-Kerem
Qumran
Zuwayzâ

Ashkelon
Beitar
VALLEY OF ELAH 3323
Bethlehem
Berekhot Shelomo
Dhîbân

Lachish
Dead Sea -1286

Gaza (Ghazzah)
Al Khalîl (Hebron)
Ein Gedi
Jad'ah

GAZA AREA (U.A.R. Adm.)

Shiqma
Massada
Al Mazra'

Khân Yûnis
Arad
Al Karak
Al Qatrañah

Beersheba
Beersheba

Tel Sharuhen
Dimona
Mamshit
Sedom (Sodom)
Al Mazâr

Gulf of Tina
Lake Bardawîl
Al 'Arîsh

Bî'r al Mazâr

Bî'r ar Rummânah

Hereidin
Tsin
Hasa

Qantarah

Shivta
Sde Boker
At Tafîlah

El 'Auja

Great Bitter Lake

Mt. Abû Qurûn 3578

GEBEL YI'ALLAR
Brûk
Jabal al Ata'Itah 5383
Jurf ad Darâwîsh

Al Quşaymah
Mahashram

Ash Shawbak

Qiraiya
Paran
Halilah

UNITED ARAB

Petrâ (Ruins)
Wâdî Mûsa

NEGEV

Ma'ân

Al Jafr

REPUBLIC

Suez
Abyâd
Ash Shâtîyah

Tawfiq
Ash Shatt
Al Kuntillah
Ra's an Naqb

An Nakhl

(EGYPT)

Sudr
Aqaba
Giraîî
3513
Aqabat al Hijâzîyah

Tareîfya
Ruâq
Timna
Jabal Ramm 5755
Ar Ramla

Ath Thamad
Eilat
Al 'Aqaba

Wardân

GEBEL EL TÎH
3789
SAUDI ARABIA

4833
QIBLIYA
Zafarânah
Abu Zanîmah
Mt. Gineina 5335

GEBEL EL IGMA

Nuwaybi 'al Muzayyinah

Gulf of Aqaba

Gulf of Suez (Khalîg el Suweis)

SINAI

COPYRIGHT BY
RAND McNALLY & COMPANY
MADE IN U.S.A.

Longitude East of Greenwich

ISRAEL   Political Map

Names of cities over 1,000,000 are capitalized

National capitals   <u>Jerusalem</u>

∴ Ancient sites and ruins

Railroads

0   10   20   30   40   50 Miles
0   20   40   60   80 Kilometers

LIFE WORLD LIBRARY

ISRAEL

TIME LIFE BOOKS ®

LIFE WORLD LIBRARY
LIFE NATURE LIBRARY
TIME READING PROGRAM
THE LIFE HISTORY OF THE UNITED STATES
LIFE SCIENCE LIBRARY
INTERNATIONAL BOOK SOCIETY
GREAT AGES OF MAN
TIME-LIFE LIBRARY OF ART
TIME-LIFE LIBRARY OF AMERICA

LIFE WORLD LIBRARY

ISRAEL

by Robert St. John

and the Editors of

TIME-LIFE BOOKS

TIME-LIFE BOOKS   NEW YORK

THE COVER: Young Israelis
stand in a wagon
at a collective settlement in the
Plain of Sharon, waiting to be
transported to work in nearby fields.

ABOUT THE WRITER

Robert St. John, author of the interpretive text for this volume of the LIFE World Library, is a veteran American correspondent and author who has an intimate knowledge of modern Israel. His acquaintanceship with foreign affairs began before World War II; his first book, *From the Land of Silent People,* an account of wartime experiences in the Balkans, was published in 1942. Since then he has published 14 others. He has written four on Israel, including *Tongue of the Prophets,* an account of the revival of Hebrew, and *Ben-Gurion, The Biography of an Extraordinary Man.* He is also the author of a biography of Egypt's president, Gamal Abdel Nasser. Widely traveled in the Middle East, he has visited Israel many times and lectures on its problems throughout the United States.

Israel © 1962, 1968 Time Inc. All rights reserved.
Published simultaneously in Canada.
Library of Congress catalogue card number 62-13962.
School and library distribution by Silver Burdett Company.

Contents

TIME-LIFE BOOKS

EDITOR
Maitland A. Edey
EXECUTIVE EDITOR
Jerry Korn
TEXT DIRECTOR   ART DIRECTOR
Martin Mann   Sheldon Cotler
CHIEF OF RESEARCH
Beatrice T. Dobie
PICTURE EDITOR
Robert G. Mason
Assistant Text Directors:
Harold C. Field, Ogden Tanner
Assistant Art Director: Arnold C. Holeywell
Assistant Chief of Research: Martha Turner

•

PUBLISHER
Rhett Austell
General Manager: Joseph C. Hazen Jr.
Planning Director: John P. Sousa III
Circulation Director: Joan D. Manley
Marketing Director: Carter Smith
Business Manager: John D. McSweeney
Publishing Board: Nicholas Benton,
Louis Bronzo, James Wendell Forbes

LIFE WORLD LIBRARY

SERIES EDITOR: Oliver E. Allen
Editorial Staff for *Israel:*
Assistant Editor: Jay Brennan
Designer: Ben Schultz
Chief Researcher: Grace Brynolson
Researchers: Paula von Haimberger Arno,
Rebecca Chaitin, Mollie Cooper, Jean Sulzberger,
Helen R. Turvey, Audry Weintrob, Linda Wolfe

EDITORIAL PRODUCTION
Color Director: Robert L. Young
Copy Staff: Marian Gordon Goldman, Ann S. Lang, Madge Raymond,
Florence Keith
Picture Department: Dolores A. Littles, Sue Bond, Marquita Jones
Art Assistants: James D. Smith, Gretchen Cassidy, John M. Woods

The text for this book was written by Robert St. John, the picture essays by Walter Karp and Peter Wood. The following individuals and departments of Time Inc. gave valuable aid in the preparation of this book: LIFE staff photographers Alfred Eisenstaedt and Paul Schutzer; Jerusalem correspondent Marlin Levin; Chief of the LIFE Picture Library, Doris O'Neil; Chief of the Bureau of Editorial Reference, Peter Draz; Chief of the TIME-LIFE News Service, Richard M. Clurman.

Introduction

Israel is a tiny country which has embarked on a great adventure. It is one in which its people feel they cannot fail. With an unshakable belief in its destiny and in the divine meaning of its existence, Israel has astounded the world with its remarkable accomplishments. But the road has been difficult.

Dishearteningly meager natural resources, severe economic pressures and constant threats to its security have magnified everyday problems. These and other conditions have combined with Israel's policy of open-armed gathering in, from all ends of the earth, Jews with sharp conflicts of outlook and wide differences of customs and social status to give Israel a special position among the nations of the world.

In one respect, Israel is a paradox. It is well known yet unknown. Although thrust into the world spotlight at the hour of its rebirth and prominent in the news ever since, its basic character remains shrouded. The long history of the Jewish people has been familiar for centuries. The wanderings and persecutions of the Jews, the Nazi atrocities, the highly successful war the Israeli military forces waged against the Arabs, beginning with their battle for independence in 1948, have focused world attention on this small democratic state. But just how the modern state of Israel came into being, what has given that nation the strength to survive and prosper, and what accounts for its influence the world over are still matters of mystery to many Americans. It is in this respect that Robert St. John and the editors of TIME-LIFE BOOKS have performed a valuable service. In both text and picture essays, modern Israel is here brought into sharp, clear focus.

An understanding of Israel must proceed from a weighing of many things. There must be consideration of Israel's history—ancient as well as modern, matters religious as well as secular, the economic as well as the political, and the people as well as the place. The new nation had scarcely come into being when its survival became imperiled. It has since lived under a perpetual threat to its existence from its Arab neighbors. Yet Israel has established in a remarkably short period of time a fabulous record of achievement in economic, social, political, scientific and cultural fields.

Of all the influences contributing to this success the most effective, perhaps, was that of the Jewish people's deep-seated dedication to religious tradition. In particular, one can trace throughout the centuries the clear outlines of orderliness, seriousness, determination and discipline which have contributed to the successful building of this young nation. One of the fundamental concepts of civilization firmly embedded in the Jewish people is the concept of law ordained by God. The early Jewish prophets were perhaps the first to call for justice in man's dealings with fellow men. Religion remains a powerful factor in shaping personal and national life. It is difficult to visit Israel without feeling a sense of religious history and spiritual reverence fall upon one like a cloak.

The latent vigor of a people who so long were unable to give full expression to their mental and physical forces has now found an opportunity for full play. This, at last, is once again their country—their homeland.

EDWARD BURNETT LAWSON
Former U.S. Ambassador to Israel

PROUD SOLDIER in the well-drilled
Israeli army is one of thousands of
women serving on active duty. Compulsory army training for both sexes
helps to mold swarms of immigrants
into Hebrew-speaking Israeli citizens.

1

The
Land
of the Book

NOWHERE on earth is there a land with
the distinctions, the problems and the potentialities of Israel. The overwhelming majority of its 2.6 million citizens are Jewish and call
themselves the People of the Book, because
their ancestors, after first settling in the area
3,500 years ago, wrote a compilation of law,
history and prophecy that came to be known as
the Bible. Their seers gave them the belief that
they were destined to become "a light unto the
nations" and to establish on this soil a civilization that would give divine meaning to existence. Twice conquerors destroyed their Temple
and dispersed them, and twice they returned,
determined to fulfill their ancient prophecies.

Twentieth Century Israel was the first nation
to be created with the approval of the world's
supreme international body, the United Nations. Its 8,000 square miles—the country is
only one quarter the size of Maine and covers
an area only one quarter of 1 per cent of that
occupied by its Arab neighbors—are so saturated with history that whenever a ditch is dug,
or the foundation for a building is excavated,
the shovels are likely to bring up relics of a
long-dead past. In partial consequence, Israel
exerts a world influence far out of proportion
to its size. More than one area of Israel is of

major religious importance to the followers of all three of the great faiths that have been born in this part of the world.

It is an oddly shaped country. On many maps the word "Israel" must be printed on the blue of the Mediterranean for lack of space on the country itself. The 1949 armistice agreements left Israel with a narrow corridor just 12 miles wide near Tel Aviv. So narrow is the country at that point that a conductor on the railroad from Jerusalem to Tel Aviv once shouted jestingly to his passengers: "Don't lean too far out the window or you'll find yourself in Jordan!" An old-fashioned prop plane can fly the country's entire length in an hour, for it is only 265 miles from the Lebanese border in the north to Eilat, the Israeli harbor on the Red Sea in the south.

If all the adult Israelis were to stand in a single line on their country's 750-mile perimeter, they would just about be able to touch fingers. Along three quarters of the 750 miles, the country faces Arab nations—Jordan, Egypt, Syria and Lebanon—which still proclaim themselves to be technically in a state of war with Israel. Although the Arab countries have declared a joint boycott against trade of any sort with Israel, exports to non-Arab lands increase annually, thanks to the country's outlets on the Mediterranean and the Red Sea.

Life is not yet all milk and honey for the people who throng the shops of Tel Aviv, climb the steep hills of Haifa, worship in the synagogues of Jerusalem and work on the land, but they seem happy to be back, finally, in the home of their ancestors. Their joy in what they call "the return" can be seen in their faces,

STAR OF DAVID, a six-pointed figure made with two interlocking triangles, is a traditional Jewish emblem that now appears on the Israeli flag.

sensed in their bearing and felt in the atmosphere of the country.

They had waited a long time for the return—19 centuries. For longer than the recorded history of many peoples they had prayed, "Next year in Jerusalem!" For generations they had repeated the words of Ezekiel, "Thus saith the Lord God, I will gather you from the people, and assemble you out of the countries where ye have been scattered and I will give you the land of Israel." Religious Jews prayed three times a day for the return. In every century Jews made perilous pilgrimages in order to set foot on the piece of land they had been promised. When the return was finally achieved, after so long a time of hope and prayer, many were stunned by the actuality of it and so they continued to speak about "next year in Jerusalem," although it was a dream no longer.

The actuality of the living dream is indeed vibrant and pulsating. Tel Aviv, Israel's largest city and the first really Jewish metropolis anywhere in the world since Biblical times, stands on what a few generations ago were barren dunes populated by foxes and jackals. For centuries the rolling dunes, swept by an often-angry wind from the sea, had known no human habitation. Today Tel Aviv is a noisy, sweating, intense, fervid city with a population of 400,000. It is the epitome of 20th Century Israel. It is a city of bright lights and brashness, culture and creativeness, noise and gaiety, ambition and defiance; a city whose people have a powerful will to live and to fulfill prophecy.

Counting those who have come in from outlying areas to do a little shopping, almost half a million people swarm the streets of Tel Aviv by day. They represent the countries to which the descendants of Abraham were scattered after the destruction of Jerusalem by the Romans in A.D. 70—the more than 100 nations of the Diaspora, or dispersal. Cock an ear and you can hear the music of Italian, the harsh tones of the Schweizerdeutsch of Switzerland, the guttural accents of Arabic, the ski's and z's of Slavic tongues, the melodiousness of Magyar, the sounds of Yiddish and Afrikaans and sometimes even of Japanese, all blended into a babble that each day becomes more and more dominated by the rich, mellow tones of modern Hebrew.

Tel Aviv also echoes to the sound of Mediterranean waves pounding on sandy beaches and rocky promontories; to the loud shouts of hawkers selling kerosene for stoves from two-wheeled carts pulled by donkeys; to the animated conversation of volatile people in canopied sidewalk cafés; the rich strains of a symphony orchestra heard through the window of an auditorium; the sad-sweet moaning of violins when a restaurant door suddenly swings open; the pounding noise of American dance music from a record player; the robust voices of young soldiers in military trucks singing pioneering songs; the minor key of a traditional religious chant intoned by a cantor in some obscure little synagogue.

The colors of Tel Aviv are the rich turquoise blue of the sea that forms the city's western boundary, the dusty green of eucalyptus trees that line the roads leading out in the other three directions, the gleaming white of tall apartment buildings and the riot of neon signs on business streets lined with shops tightly jammed together. The smells of the city are as diverse as its colors, with the enticing aroma of freshly roasted coffee mingling with the pervasive odor of cooking oils and the nutlike scent of sweet corn being boiled over charcoal on numberless street corner stands.

The sense of excitement which all visitors feel in Tel Aviv is compounded by the fact that it has more art galleries, more espresso shops and cafés, more theaters, more libraries and bookshops than can be discovered in any other city in the Middle East—more, perhaps, than in any city of comparable size anywhere in the world.

MENORAH, a seven-branched candelabrum, has been a holy symbol of Judaism since the time of Moses. It appears on the Israeli state seal.

There are almost a thousand cafés, restaurants and snack bars. Each, like an English pub, caters to a specific clientele. There is the café of the journalists, the café of the barristers, the café where those of a certain minor political group always meet and the café to which an architect will take an important client to discuss plans for a new building. There is a rendezvous patronized mostly by short-bearded intellectuals, and one in which waiters and clients nearly all speak the dialect of a particular remote area beyond the Caucasus.

In Tel Aviv there are seven repertory theaters open the year round; the Philharmonic has a 10-month season, and on the newsstands are 26 Israeli daily newspapers, printed in 12 different languages. One street alone, Allenby Road—named after the British general who liberated Palestine from the Turks in World War I—has more than 100 bookshops and bookstalls. Besides books the shops carry copies of the 400 weekly, fortnightly, monthly and quarterly Israeli magazines. Nearly 2,000 new books are published annually within the country, and each year a considerable amount of foreign exchange is released for the import of literature from abroad.

Tel Aviv has its Coney Island, a short stretch along the beach where hawkers sell slices of bright red watermelon, colored ice water and an Arab version of hamburgers—*falafel*, a purse-shaped sandwich of dough filled with what look like deep-fried meat balls; the balls are actually made of mashed chickpeas. The city also has a national opera company, several new first-rate hotels, modern shopping centers, high-rise apartments facing the Mediterranean, and a growing university. One special phenomenon is that Tel Aviv also has more medical men than it needs. The average for the United States is one doctor for every 750 inhabitants. In Israel over recent years a flood of European refugees—including many professional men—has brought the little country's average to one doctor for every 440 persons. Some have been converted into farmers and factory workers, but many of the rest have settled in Tel Aviv and become specialists, advertising for patients with signs that have sometimes been bizarre ("Doctor for women and other diseases").

Close beside Tel Aviv—and now part of the same municipality—is ancient Jaffa, in whose harbor Jonah began his famous voyage. Most of Jaffa's Arabs fled during the fighting of 1948, when Israel was invaded by Arab armies after the withdrawal of the British. Its population is now primarily Jewish, but the old quarter still resembles an Arab city, with twisting, cobbled streets and a market where exotic pieces of jewelry can still be bought cheaply.

SIXTY miles up the coast from Tel Aviv is Haifa, in the area where the prophet Elijah called down fire from the heavens to consume an offering to the Lord. The city has been built at three levels on Mount Carmel, the "Vineyard of God." Americans often remark about Haifa, "Doesn't it remind you of San Francisco?" and Europeans say, "Very much like Naples." Once Haifa was a quiet Arab fishing village; today it is the country's principal seaport. Ships flying the flags of almost all of the maritime nations put in there. It is the home port of a growing merchant fleet and has facilities for large liners. Haifa's tallest building, a 191-foot grain elevator, stands at the water's edge. At water level also are factories, automobile assembly plants and oil refineries. Halfway up Mount Carmel are shops, movie theaters, offices and modest apartment buildings. At the top of the mountain are de luxe hotels, night clubs and the homes of those who have prospered. The view is breathtaking from the summit, the crescent-shaped harbor exciting the dreamer and the poet in many Israelis. From the mountaintop on a clear day it is even possible to see the snow-capped peak of Mount Hermon, 70 miles away on the Syria-Lebanon border.

WHILE Tel Aviv is Israel's metropolis of gaiety and smart commercialism, and Haifa its showpiece of industrial progress, good architecture, jewel-like parks and intelligent city planning, Jerusalem is the real heart and spirit of Israel. Down through the ages this ancient capital city has meant more to more people than any other human dwelling place. Men of the Stone Age lived on the site and worshiped nature. Neolithic men armed with weapons of polished flint battled over the area with warriors who still used rocks as weapons. Since then the rocky approaches to Jerusalem have been stained with the blood of millions of men who fought in the name of a religion or of nationalism, or merely because of some tyrant's lust for power. Canaanites, Amorites, Egyptians, Babylonians, Persians, Greeks, Syrians, Romans, Crusaders, Saracens, Frenchmen, Germans, Austrians, Turks, the British—all at one time or another fought over what Jews, Christians and Moslems alike today call the Holy City. There David and Solomon ruled, Jesus taught and suffered, and Mohammed is believed to have ascended to heaven.

Under the terms of the 1947 United Nations plan for the partition of Palestine, Jerusalem was to have become an international city. But in the fighting that broke out six months before the British left in 1948, it became the scene of bloody battles between Israeli and Arab forces. The struggle ended with the Arabs holding the Old City, in which are most of the shrines of all three religions, and the Israelis holding the New City, which in 1948 they made their capital. In the six-day war with the Arabs, in June 1967, Israel occupied the Old City. Within days its administration was integrated with that of the New City, and all traces of the barbed wire, mines and check points that had kept Jerusalem divided were removed. For the first time since 1948, Jews were again able to pray at the Old City's Wailing Wall, the sole part of Solomon's Temple surviving the second destruction in 70 A.D.

In the intervening years the New City had in many ways taken over the pious traditions of the Old. It is the center of Orthodox tradition. Through its streets walk bearded, long-coated Jews whose curled locks swing under broad-brimmed hats. In Mea Shearim, the ultra-Orthodox religious quarter, there are almost no people on the streets at certain hours: the inhabitants are praying in the synagogues. Jerusalem is totally different from Tel Aviv. It lies "in high places amid mountains," as the Old Testament relates. It is in fact Israel's most striking city, particularly at night, when its buildings stand outlined in moonlight against the ancient hills from which God is said to have taken the dust that formed Adam. "When the world was created, it received ten measures of beauty," says the Talmud, the oral tradition of Judaism. "Nine fell on Jerusalem . . . one on the rest of the earth."

TODAY pious and non-pious Jews alike are flocking to Jerusalem. They are young men, who come not to die but to live and create. Out of Jerusalem's pinkish-yellow stone they have erected massive public buildings, religious academies, hospitals, the Hebrew University and even supermarkets. The Judean hills, which have been brown and desolate for centuries, are now growing greener each year with trees, vines and small farms. New villages are scattered across the landscape. The country all about is

By the rivers of Babylon,
There we sat down, yea, we wept,
When we remembered Zion.
Upon the willows in the midst thereof
We hanged up our harps.
For there they that led us captive
*   asked of us words of song,*
And our tormentors asked of us mirth:
"Sing us one of the songs of Zion."

How shall we sing the Lord's song
In a foreign land?
If I forget thee, O Jerusalem,
Let my right hand forget her cunning.
Let my tongue cleave to the roof
*   of my mouth,*
If I remember thee not;
If I set not Jerusalem
Above my chiefest joy.

LIVING SPIRIT of Israel's people both in ancient and contemporary times is evoked by the fervent, dedicated lines of the 137th Psalm, reproduced in part here.

13

rapidly being transformed into a semblance of what it was at the height of Jerusalem's glory.

Some aspects of Israel remain largely unchanged. On Lake Kinneret, the body of water to the north also known as the Sea of Galilee, fish are still caught much as they were in the days when Christ persuaded the two Galileans, Simon Peter and Andrew, to change their vocations and become fishers of men. Yet here too there are many new villages along the shores of the lake, and the old city of Tiberias has become a fashionable resort. At Ein-Gev on the eastern shore, within range of the guns that pointed toward Israel from Syria, a music festival was initiated that is now held each year and attracts performers and enthusiastic audiences from all over the world.

The Negev, the desert to the south, contains more than half of Israel's total land area; its northern reaches are gradually being reclaimed for agriculture. Eilat, the Red Sea port near the spot where the Queen of Sheba's ships dropped anchor when they arrived with gifts for King Solomon, has developed from a forlorn spot marked by a single mud-brick police outpost into a thriving city. It offers handsome hotels for tourists, glass-bottom boats for viewing marine life and a desalinization plant that may someday help to realize the ancient dream of using sea water to irrigate the desert.

A few miles to the north of Eilat are Solomon's copper mines, which are being worked again by Jews as they were 3,000 years ago. The exported copper is a minor source of revenue from abroad, but the revitalization of this Biblical industry has been of major symbolic importance to the young nation.

EVERYWHERE these purposeful people are changing the face of the land. Israelis seem unaware that the phrase for "not possible" even exists in their language. Their belief in modern miracles began in 1948 with their victories over the Arab armies. They proudly call the struggle the War of Liberation, and their victory has led to the often repeated remark: "He who does not believe in miracles in Israel is no realist." Typical of the spirit that motivates present-day Israelis is the story of the young pioneers who, before Israel became a state, founded a cooperative settlement south of Jericho on the Dead Sea shore. In spite of the fact that experts said that nothing would grow in the saline soil of the area, they washed it repeatedly with fresh water until they succeeded in removing most of the salt. Then they began planting. Crops flourished in the washed soil.

THE transformation in Israel is illustrated by a well-known story told of a guide who, asked by a tourist about a large building they were passing, glanced at it and replied, "I am sorry, madam, but I have no idea what it is. I haven't been in this part of the country for the last several weeks."

Everywhere in this ancient place, the present recalls the past. In the Valley of Elah, where David slew Goliath, there is now a village of immigrants from Yemen. From the summit of Mount Tabor, where Deborah stood with her forces against the Canaanites and the transfiguration of Christ occurred, there is a magnificent view of the prosperous settlements of the Jezreel Valley. Near Massada, on the Dead Sea in the Wilderness of Judah, where Jewish soldiers made a final stand in Judea against the Romans in 73 A.D., a youth hostel has been erected. In the Valley of Ayalon, where Joshua commanded the moon to stand still, a dam has been built to collect the great quantities of water that rush down the Judean hills during the rainy season. Beersheba, where Abraham planted a tamarisk tree, has become a city of factories, hotels and hospitals and the bustling capital of the Negev.

The past, the present and the future dissolve into each other everywhere. At Caesarea, tourists play on Israel's first golf course. Nearby, archaeologists with specially designed underwater equipment search the floor of the harbor for relics of King Herod's time. In the distance, replacing earlier immigrant camps, rise white-walled cottages and apartment houses for the Israelis of today and tomorrow.

In one of bustling Tel Aviv's numerous cafés, Israeli youths while away an evening talking amiably over coffee, a favorite pastime.

Western Dynamo in the Land of Zion

Israel, it has been said, is a land of unlimited impossibilities. Smaller than Massachusetts and half desert, it cannot yet support itself economically, but it spends large sums to bring in immigrants. A land created by idealism, it suffers from conflicting ideals—religious orthodoxy and secular democracy; a zeal for pioneer heroism and a desire for security. But Israel does have one incalculable asset—its citizens' energetic delight in merely being alive in Zion.

15

ECSTATIC PIETISTS dance near a shrine during a religious holiday (*opposite*). Customarily bearded, the men belong to a devout Jewish group known as the Hassidim.

TOURING SCHOOL CHILDREN in Jerusalem gaze proudly at a huge bronze *menorah* (ritual candelabrum), a gift from Britain that now stands in front of the Knesset.

SALT-THICK WATERS of the Dead Sea buoy up a woman as though she were a cork. The sun-scorched lake, lying 1,286 feet below sea level, is a valuable source of potash.

HALLOWED LAKE, the little Sea of Galilee provides a quiet retreat for vacationers (*below*). The mineral springs near the lake were a resort spot even in Roman times.

HARD-WON GROVES of olives surround a village in Galilee. The hillside terraces, laboriously built up in recent years on long-neglected land, recall Biblical days when the area was famed for its olive groves. The village is inhabited by Druses, an Arabic-speaking people who practice an esoteric religion peculiar to themselves.

GAY AWNINGS that clamp down over the ubiquitous little sun porches are a household necessity in hot and humid Tel Aviv.

RESIDENTIAL AREA of Tel Aviv (*below*) has characteristic rows of three-story apartment buildings separated by air spaces.

SUNNY CITIES along the coast combine Mediterranean styles with modernism

COASTAL RESORT of Herzliya is dotted with new luxury hotels whose suntanned guests radiate an aura of deep comfort. A fashionable gathering place and tourist attraction a few miles up the coast from Tel Aviv, the city, named after the founder of modern Zionism, Theodore Herzl, boasts one of the country's finest beaches.

THE HOLY CITY of Jerusalem, cherished sanctuary of three great religions, bears the marks of an immensely long and turbulent history

A MEDIEVAL WALL surrounds Old Jerusalem, a city that was already ancient in the 10th Century B.C. when King David proclaimed it the capital of Israel. Seen from a point outside the Damascus Gate *(right),* the Old City reflects the ebb and flow of warring armies and hostile creeds—as well as changing architectural styles—that followed its first Jewish flowering. The minarets of Moslem mosques jut up here and there, while the tall, pointed tower *(far right)* tops the Christian Church of the Redeemer. Following the 1967 war, the Old City once again came under Jewish control, though its Jewish heritage lies largely hidden in old foundations like the Wailing Wall, which ironically forms part of a wall surrounding Islam's great, golden Dome of the Rock, a Seventh Century mosque *(upper left).*

RADIANT PANELS representing the 12 tribes of Israel were done by Marc Chagall for the Hadassah-Hebrew University Medical Center synagogue. Hadassah, an organization of American Jewish women, commissioned them.

2

A
Highway
of History

ISRAEL is the only nation in the world which employs the Old Testament as its history textbook, and it does so with rightful pride. The stories recounted for hundreds of years by seers and singers before they were written down to become chapters in the books of the Bible constitute an epochal tale of a great and extraordinary people—of their origins some 3,500 years ago in the lower Tigris-Euphrates valley, of their wanderings through the Mediterranean area today known as the Fertile Crescent, of their triumphs and travails in Egypt, of their liberator and teacher Moses, of their establishment of a powerful empire

under David and Solomon, and of their eventual conquest by pagan Rome. The story is, of course, a familiar one, known not only to Jews and Christians, but to peoples of many other faiths. To Moslems, both Abraham and Moses are precursors of Mohammed, the prophet who declared that Allah was the only God; to Buddhists, Moses is a trail breaker who heralded the coming of their own messenger from God, the Gautama Buddha.

Yet the Old Testament remains of paramount importance to modern Israel. This extraordinary work is not only the history of ancient Israel and a document of deep religious significance. It is the key to an understanding of the establishment of the 20th Century nation. "Unto thy seed," says the Lord God to Abraham, in Genesis, "will I give this land." To this day, there is dispute among Biblical critics about "Abraham." To some, he is a single historical character. To others "Abraham" is a general term used by the original oral authors of the Bible to identify different leaders at different periods. For 20th Century Israel, the question does not particularly matter. Sometime in the second millennium B.C., Abraham—or the people of Abraham—were promised "the land of Canaan" by their God, and Abraham and his people entered into a covenant of faith and devotion to God. The Promised Land does not precisely conform to the boundaries of present-day Israel, but it lies within the same area. Indeed, because of the Biblical covenant, modern Israel could not be elsewhere. In 1903, for example, when Zionism —the movement which eventually brought Israel into being—was gathering force, a sympathetic British government suggested to Zionist leaders that it might offer them an area for Jewish resettlement in East Africa. The offer was rejected; only in the land promised to Abraham, they said, could Israel be reborn.

THE people of Abraham were originally idol-worshipers who emigrated from the ancient city of Ur, near the Persian Gulf, to the city of Haran, in what is now Turkey. It was there that Abraham rejected his fathers' gods and set off with his own flocks to lead an independent life. Spurred by the heavenly command to found a nation of people who would serve a single deity, he traveled west from Haran, then south until he reached the Promised Land of Canaan, a place of plains, mountains and valleys lying roughly between the River Jordan, the Dead Sea and the Mediterranean. In it he found walled cities inhabited by Semitic peoples. The Canaanites called Abraham the *Ibri* and his fellow nomads *Ibrim* ("from the other side") because they had come from across a river—probably the Euphrates. From *Ibri* was

born the word Hebrew. Abraham itself means "father of many." After Abraham's death, his son Isaac settled in southern Canaan, constructed cisterns in the Negev desert and grew rich. To him, the Bible relates, God renewed the promise that Canaan would belong to Abraham's heirs.

Isaac had twin sons, Esau and Jacob. Jacob, the younger, disguised himself as Esau and thus obtained the blessing of his aged, blind father. Fleeing Esau's wrath after his trickery, Jacob was nevertheless blessed by his God. On the way to his mother's people in Mesopotamia, he had a vision of angels ascending and descending a ladder to the heavens. Later, he spent a night in a dark canyon wrestling with his own soul, which appeared in the form of a mysterious stranger. After that Jacob was called Israel, a name which means "He who strove with God." The 12 sons he sired were accordingly known as the "children of Israel" and the families they founded became the 12 tribes of Israel. Jacob also was promised the land of Canaan by the God of Abraham.

The favorite of Jacob's—or Israel's—12 sons was Joseph. The Bible relates that his jealous brothers sold him into slavery in Egypt. But his honesty, wisdom and personality earned Joseph the right to rule Egypt as the Pharaoh's chief minister. When famine in Canaan drove his brothers to Egypt in search of food, Joseph sent for his father also and obtained land for all of them. For a period the Jews lived unmolested in Egypt. But some time after Joseph's death a new Pharaoh ordered all the Hebrews enslaved.

IT was in this captivity that the towering figure of the Old Testament arose. The Biblical story says that Moses, the son of Hebrew parents, was hidden in the reeds along the Nile by his mother, after Pharaoh had ordered all Hebrew male infants slain. Found and adopted by the daughter of the Pharaoh, he was educated at the Egyptian court, only to be called by God to redeem the covenant of Abraham and to lead the Israelites back to the Promised Land of Canaan. After Egypt had been visited by plagues, Pharaoh permitted the slaves to leave. What came to be known as the Exodus followed. Moses led the Israelites across the Sinai Peninsula until they came to Mount Sinai. At the summit God revealed Himself to Moses and gave him the Ten Commandments and the laws which became the foundation of the Judaic—and Christian—code. He received, also, a renewed order to lead his people back to Canaan and there to create "a holy nation."

BUT the time had not yet come, nor were the people ready. Moses and his followers wandered around the inhospitable desert for 40 years, until a strong and defiant new generation, which had not known slavery in Egypt, was ready to battle for the land that God had long ago told Abraham was to be theirs.

Now Moses led them back. The route of the return was north through what are now the Negev and Jordan to Mount Nebo. There Moses, now 120 years old, again climbed to a mountain summit and again heard the voice of God, who showed him all the land of Gilead, all Naphtali, the land of Ephraim and Manasseh, Judah "unto the utmost sea" and the valley of Jericho, explaining that this was the land He had promised to Abraham, Isaac and Jacob. But because he had rebelled against God's command in the desert of Zin, Moses was himself forbidden to enter Canaan. "I have caused thee to see it with thine eyes, but thou shalt not go over thither," the Lord said to Moses.

The death of the aged prophet occurred immediately after this event. Joshua, Moses' lieutenant, took command and led the Israelites across the Jordan River, stormed and captured Jericho and eventually conquered most of Canaan, which he divided among the 12 tribes.

In their first two centuries in Canaan, the Israelites were ruled by a succession of "judges" who were sometimes military heroes and sometimes judicial officials. All claimed divine inspiration. One of the most celebrated of the judges was Samson, who fought his most famous battles against the Philistines, an aggressive people in southwestern Canaan. He was betrayed by the Philistine woman Delilah, then was captured, blinded and taken to Gaza, one of the Philistines' fortified cities. In a sudden resurgence of strength he pulled down the enemy's temple with his bare hands.

Enemies continued to press in on the Israelites from all sides and the 12 tribes decided to band together and set up a joint monarchy. The first Jewish king, a peasant-warrior named Saul, was a tragic figure. He spent most of his life fighting—and generally defeating—the Philistines, only to become embittered in his later years by the popularity of a young shepherd named David. David won wide acclaim by defeating a Philistine giant, Goliath of Gath. The David-Goliath encounter is the Bible's most spectacular duel. First David felled his opponent with a well-aimed shot from a sling; then he decapitated him with the Philistine's own sword. David fell in love with Michal, one of Saul's daughters, and married her. Spiritual and gifted, he also became the king's personal musician, with the task of playing softly on his harp to calm the monarch whenever Saul became the victim of one of his periodic spells of mental depression. For years the king unsuccessfully plotted the death of his young son-in-law, then was himself wounded in battle by an enemy arrow. To avoid capture, he committed suicide by falling on his sword.

David was crowned Saul's successor. Early in his reign, he decided to make an easily defendable hilltop town, then probably called Salem and ruled by a people known as the Jebusites, into his capital. David took it by sending his men into Salem through a tunnel normally used for water. Heretofore unimportant, the place before long began to be celebrated as Jerusalem, the city of David, poet and conqueror.

THE country reached its greatest prosperity and glory under Solomon, David's son. Solomon brought in architects and builders from Phoenicia to fashion for him a temple of stone, precious metal and rare woods, the first holy building of the Israelites. Two cherubim carved from olive wood guarded the holy Ark of the

Covenant, in which were kept the sacred stone tablets that had long ago been delivered by God to Moses on the Sinai mountaintop.

The temple was only the start of Solomon's building program. Because he had a thousand wives and concubines, he had an obvious need of many palaces. He constructed the most magnificent for his favorite wife, the daughter of the Egyptian Pharaoh. He also built roads and aqueducts throughout the land. Under him, Israel became a powerful nation.

Oceangoing vessels brought from Africa and India cargoes of spices, precious metals, ivory and animals. Near what is now the Red Sea port of Eilat furnaces were built to smelt copper and iron. So much precious metal arrived from abroad as tribute that Solomon ordered golden shields made for his soldiers. One of his biographers wrote that he "exceeded all the kings of the earth for riches and for wisdom." Yet his critics accused him of betraying the moral precepts of his own religion out of his egotistical love of power and splendor.

AFTER Solomon's death, his empire was torn by internal dissension. The 10 tribes in the north revolted against Rehoboam, the son who had succeeded to the throne, and picked a king of their own. The two southern tribes retained Jerusalem as their capital and called their kingdom Judah, from which the word Jew was eventually derived.

Some 200 years after Solomon's death, the northern kingdom fell to the armies of the aggressive and expanding empire of Assyria and its population was scattered throughout the Middle East. Thus the Ten Lost Tribes, as they came to be known, vanished from history.

The southern kingdom of Judah, however, maintained a precarious independence for another 135 years. But the kingdom was no longer powerful, and it was in this period that the great prophet Isaiah began to warn of disaster. "They that forsake the Lord," he said, "shall be consumed." In 598 B.C., Jerusalem was captured by King Nebuchadnezzar of Babylon, and in 586 the walls of the city were torn down, and the Temple was burned. Most of the Judeans were taken to Babylon, but instead of vanishing from history through intermarriage and assimilation, as the Israelites of the northern kingdom had done, they listened to the advice of their prophet Jeremiah, who urged them to keep alive their Jewishness. In Babylon, guided by the prophet Ezekiel, they prayed earnestly for the day of the Return. Half a century later Babylon fell to King Cyrus of Persia, who issued a decree permitting the Jews to go back to Judah. Thousands did return. Grandchildren of many who had been taken into captivity began reconstructing the Temple. This was the event which is referred to by Jews today as "the first Return."

When Alexander of Macedon and his armies swept across the Middle East in the Fourth Century B.C., he ordered that the Temple be spared and the Jews left unmolested. But nearly 200 years later, a Syrian conqueror named Antiochus Epiphanes forbade them to observe the practices of Judaic Law, and defiled the Temple by ordering therein sacrifices to Greek gods. In 167 B.C. a small army of rebels led by Judah Maccabee, son of an aged Jewish priest, drove the Syrians out of Jerusalem. When regular services began again after the Temple had been purified, the *menorah*, the holy candelabrum of seven branches, was lighted in the Temple. Miraculously, it burned for eight days

GREAT EVENTS IN A HISTORIC CITY

Some epochal events that have taken place in Jerusalem are shown opposite, superimposed on a drawing of the Old City. Near the east wall of the Old City, Abraham prepared to sacrifice Isaac (1). David (2) made Jerusalem ancient Israel's capital. Christ's last days, beginning with the Last Supper (3) and ending in the descent from the Cross (6), were spent in Jerusalem. The Wailing Wall is a remnant of the Second Temple, destroyed in A.D. 70 (7). From the Dome of the Rock, Mohammed departed for heaven (8). The first Crusaders (9) entered near the Storks' Tower.

OLD CITY

OLD & NEW JERUSALEM

DAMASCUS GATE

HEROD'S GATE

STORKS' TOWER

ST. STEPHEN'S GATE

GOLDEN GATE

JAFFA RD.

NEW GATE

KING SOLOMON'S ST.

VIA DOLOROSA

DAMASCUS ST.

HOLY SEPULCHRE

CHRISTIAN ST.

WAILING WALL

DOME OF THE ROCK

JAFFA GATE

DAVID ST.

ST. OF THE CHAIN

BAZAAR OF THE JEWS

CITADEL

DUNG GATE

ZION GATE

COENACULUM

1	Abraham's sacrifice	6	Descent from the Cross
2	King David playing harp	7	Destruction of the Temple
3	The Last Supper	8	Ascension of Mohammed
4	Flagellation of Christ	9	The first Crusaders
5	Ecce homo ("Behold the man")		

Arno

on a one-day supply of oil. The miracle of the "Eternal Light" is still celebrated every year during the eight-day Jewish feast of Hanukkah, or dedication.

For the next hundred years the Jews prospered under the Maccabees. Then came the Romans. In 63 B.C. Judah became a Roman satellite, which the Romans called Judea. Years later Herod the Great was given the official title of "King of the Jews." He made a show place of the seaport of Caesarea and expanded and refurbished the Temple, but shortly before his death he became so obsessed with a fear of assassination that he executed everyone he suspected of plotting against him. Most scholars believe that he was the ruler who ordered the extermination of all the Jewish children in Bethlehem two years of age or less; the Gospel of Saint Matthew relates that the decision was prompted by Herod's having been told by wise men of the birth there of a Jewish child whom they called "King of the Jews."

HEROD went to his death when Jesus was still a child. It was some 30 years later that Jesus made the famous entry into Jerusalem. His followers believed that Jesus was the Messiah, "the anointed one" who, Judaic tradition said, would deliver men from oppression and bring them salvation. But Jesus was not accepted as the Messiah by the Jews. His extraordinary life and death, however, created a new, non-Jewish religion and made the Jewish homeland of vital importance to a second great religion.

The Jews continued their own way.

In A.D. 66 the Jews of Judea began a general revolt, defying the military might of the entire Roman Empire. The Roman proconsul Vespasian sent legions sweeping across the country. In A.D. 70 his son and successor Titus overpowered Jerusalem, burned the Temple to the ground, slaughtered indiscriminately and sold thousands of Jews into slavery.

For more than 60 years Jewish worship was forbidden, but in A.D. 132 a new Hebrew hero, Shimon Bar-Kokhba, led half a million Jews against the Romans. Many thousands of soldiers and civilians were killed before Bar-Kokhba and his followers were finally defeated in a last stand at Beitar, a fortified hill not far from Jerusalem.

This time the Romans made sure that rebellion would not break out again. Almost all of the surviving Jews were scattered throughout the empire. The word Judea was obliterated from all maps. From then on the land was known as Syria Palestina, after the most detested of the Jews' ancient enemies, the Philistines.

THE era of exile had now begun. Yet the Jews still retained their identity as a people. Their academies in Babylon and Palestine completed a detailed commentary on the Old Testament, known as the Talmud, which set the pattern of later Jewish life and law. In some of the countries in which they sought sanctuary, the Jews were welcomed because of their knowledge of trade, science and the arts. But the intense religious fervor which stimulated and accompanied the Crusaders' efforts to liberate the Holy Land from the Arabs in turn generated an unfortunate by-product: an increase in bigotry. During the Middle Ages, England and France expelled their Jews. Spain and Portugal later followed suit. Elsewhere in Europe Jews were legislated against, forced to dwell only in certain crowded city sections called ghettos, deprived of normal civil rights and often massacred or forcibly baptized.

Meanwhile, Palestine year by year became more and more a denuded, eroded wilderness. It was invaded and occupied by Arabs in 636, Crusaders in 1099, Tatars in 1244 and Turks in 1517. But for none of them did it become a homeland tied to prophecy, vision and hope.

It remained so for the homeless Jews. Three times a day during their prayers, in the many countries of their exile, the dispersed Jews would repeat the words: "Sound the great horn for our freedom, lift up the banner to gather our exiles and gather us from the four corners of the earth to our land." But it was to be a long wait—almost 2,000 years—before the ancient dream would become reality.

In the Polish city of Cracow, women trudge down a medieval-looking alley that runs crookedly through the quarter reserved for Jews.

Final Moments in the Epoch of Exile

For 2,000 years the real history of Israel concerned people who were not even there. It was the story of the Diaspora, the long period when the vast majority of Jews had to live in nations and empires not their own. Today the old life of the Diaspora has largely disappeared. But before it vanished, a Russian-born American named Roman Vishniac recorded the ghetto communities (segregated Jewish quarters) of eastern Europe as they were in 1939. His pictures, shown on these pages, do not survey the entire Jewish dispersion, but they have captured the peculiar intensity and fragility that characterized the exile's lot wherever he lived.

31

THE GHETTOS *were cramped and bleak, but their people saw them as havens*

ON A COBBLED STREET in the Slovak city of Bratislava, schoolboys wend their way home past dingy tenements.

PAST A SHANTY a Lublin housewife returns from market (*left*). A drab poverty was the usual ghetto condition.

IN A DOORWAY beyond the confines of the ghetto (*opposite*), peddlers ply their wares on a Warsaw street.

INTENSELY INGROWN and welded together

by a shared religious faith, the communities of eastern Europe

were largely cut off from outside influences

until the holocaust of Nazism swept over them

HUDDLING TOGETHER, some of Cracow's 72,000 Jews stand near a sign reminding them to light holiday candles. In 1939 the Cracow ghetto was 600 years old.

TURNING THE CORNER of a street in the Cracow ghetto, an old man in a greatcoat treads the slushy snow. The Cracow Jewish community was obliterated by the Nazis.

In 1912, members of Degania, Israel's oldest communal village, celebrate completion of the first permanent building in the settlement.

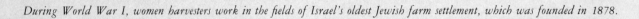

During World War I, women harvesters work in the fields of Israel's oldest Jewish farm settlement, which was founded in 1878.

EARLY PIONEERS in the drive to re-settle Palestine arrived before World War I to set up crude farm villages wherever they were allowed to buy land. Most of these hardy idealists had never practiced farming before.

3

An Ancient Prophecy Fulfilled

THE hope of the Jewish people for a land of their own was sometimes strained during the 1,878 years between the destruction of the Second Temple and the re-creation of Israel. Millions of Jews all over the world were prayerfully confident that Jerusalem would be restored to them only when the Messiah—the ultimate savior—arrived. They reproached themselves, saying in their intercessions with God, "But on account of our sins we were exiled from our land and removed far from our country." They showed their impatient longing in their constant prayers: "Rebuild it [Jerusalem] soon in our days as an everlasting building, and speedily set up therein the throne of David."

At no time during the centuries of exile was Palestine ever devoid of Jews, although their number varied from era to era. During the Turkish rule, which began in the 16th Century, many of Jerusalem's permanent Jewish residents were zealously religious men who spent their waking hours sitting close to the few stones that were left of the Temple—the Wailing Wall —reciting their lamentations. Apart from them, the Holy Land was populated largely by Arabs.

Jewish pilgrims coming from abroad to die— to be close to the Holy Temple on resurrection day—would heed the old tradition to recite, on seeing the devastation of their holy city, the words, "Zion has become a desert, Jerusalem a wilderness," and to tear a finger's breadth of a garment, coat, jacket or shirt.

But later there were others who came to live and to resurrect the land. The rise of liberalism, of romanticism and of nationalism in 19th Century Europe all affected the Jews of the time. Chaim Weizmann, the elegant and astute research chemist who would later become the new state of Israel's first president, described the mood of the Jewish masses in Russia at the turn of the century: "An impulse arose, vague, groping, unformulated, for Jewish self-liberation. It was genuinely of the folk; it was saturated with Jewish tradition; and it was connected with the most ancient memories of the land where Jewish life had first expressed itself in freedom." During a wave of fierce pogroms (mass violence against Jews) in eastern Europe in the 1880s, many Jews fled to America, while a few dozen idealistic young intellectuals in Russia formed a back-to-Zion agricultural movement which they called BILU, from the Hebrew initials of the Biblical phrase, "House of Jacob, come, let us go!" They took an oath to work on the land; then the more daring set out for Palestine.

ALONG with several hundred other members of the Lovers of Zion movement, they formed the First Aliyah—a word literally meaning ascent, the Hebrew term for immigration. They went ashore at Jaffa by bribing Turkish officials to overlook in their case the newly imposed ban on Jewish immigration. Then, frustrated by the problems of founding an agricultural colony of their own, they became day laborers. Hard work, the inhospitable climate, malaria and attacks by marauders sent many of the young idealists to their graves or back to Russia. "Awlad al Mout"—Children of Death —the Arabs called them. But a beginning had been made. The First Aliyah had planted roots in the Palestinian soil.

By an odd twist of circumstance, the loudest and clearest voice then calling the Jews together from the Diaspora, or Dispersion, was that of a Budapest-born lawyer and journalist who at one time had been so indifferent a Jew that he felt mass conversion to Christianity might be the answer to pogroms and anti-Semitism. Once he became struck with the idea of a Jewish homeland, Theodor Herzl put all his fiery energy into publicizing it. His book, *The Jewish State; An Attempt at a Modern Solution of the Jewish Question*, was published in Vienna in 1896.

HERZL'S writings and political negotiations gave tremendous impetus to the movement which the world in the next half century would come to know well as Zionism. According to his original conception, there should be an orderly exodus of Jews to some unspecified homeland, the movement to take place under the aegis of the major European powers, most of which would—Herzl assumed—welcome having part of their Jewish population drained away. From the outset there was opposition to Herzl's scheme among Jews, forming the basis of a controversy which still persists. Wealthy and influential Jews who had assimilated themselves in European countries and the U.S., and who felt that Jews everywhere would be better off if they did not stress their Jewishness, were the most prominent of the anti-Zionists. Reform Jews (the liberal wing of Judaism) considered the whole idea retrograde. Many Orthodox Jews objected strongly to Herzl's proposal since they believed that only with the arrival of the Messiah would the Jews be called together again.

Despite this criticism, Herzl's writings appealed to the mass of Jews in eastern Europe, and in 1897 he called a congress in Switzerland of Jewish representatives from all over the world. By this time Herzl had come to accept the eastern European Jews' insistence on Palestine as the movement's target, and the congress drew up a program for "the creation in Palestine of a home for the Jewish people secured by public law." Later a Jewish National Fund was set up to purchase land in Palestine as the property of the entire Jewish people.

The resumption of pogroms in Russia and the failure of the democratic movement there helped to produce the Second Aliyah, which brought 50,000 European Jews to Palestine between 1904 and the start of World War I. Many were socialist Labor Zionists who wanted to create in Palestine a new kind of society and a new kind of Jew by dignifying toil on the land. Again they suffered from epidemics and from attacks by the Arabs, and also from exploitation by Jewish landowners who appeared to them to be more interested in paying the lowest possible wages than in bright dreams of Zion. Not all of them were idealists and not all stayed. But a few thousand were dedicated pioneers. David Ben-Gurion, a young Polish Jew who became one of the founders of modern Israel, was among them. He wrote:

"The spirit of my childhood and my dreams had triumphed and was joyous! I was in the Land of Israel, in a Jewish village. . . . The howling of jackals in the vineyards; the braying of donkeys in the stables . . . the murmur of the distant sea; the darkening shadows of the groves; the enchantment of stars in the deep blue; the faraway skies, drowsily bright—everything intoxicated me."

After his arrival in the Galilean village of Sejera, where he worked in the fields and helped set up the first Jewish armed watchmen's organization, he wrote, "Here I found the environment that I had sought so long. No shopkeepers or speculators, no non-Jewish hirelings or idlers living on the labor of others. . . . These were villagers, smelling wholesomely of midden and the ripening ear, and burnt by the sun."

FAR from Palestine's soil a leading role in early Zionism was played by Chaim Weizmann, who was instrumental in winning British espousal of the Zionist cause. Early in World War I, when the Allies were suffering catastrophic military reverses, Britain had given the Arabs sweeping but unspecific promises of a unified independent Arab state if they would help defeat the Turkish Empire, which was allied with Germany. Then on November 2, 1917, in a letter from Foreign Secretary Arthur James Balfour to Lord Rothschild, a leader of the Anglo-Jewish community, Britain came out wholeheartedly for the Zionist aims:

"His Majesty's Government," the letter reported, "view with favour the establishment in Palestine of a national home for the Jewish people, and will use their best endeavours to facilitate the achievement of this object, it being clearly understood that nothing shall be done which may prejudice the civil and religious rights of existing non-Jewish communities in Palestine, or the rights and political status enjoyed by Jews in any other country."

The Balfour Declaration was to a large extent the product of genuine humanitarian feelings. But it was too vague: what is a "national home," and how would the rights of non-Jews be protected? From this well-meaning pronouncement grew some 30 years of trouble between Britain and the Arabs.

A FEW weeks after the issuance of the Declaration, British General Sir Edmund Allenby defeated the Turks at Jerusalem. Almost a year later the Turks were driven from Galilee as well. In April 1920, at the Italian seaport resort of San Remo, the Allies met to hand out the spoils. There, Great Britain was assigned the League of Nations Mandate for Palestine. The Balfour pledge was incorporated in the terms of the Mandate, which recognized "the historical connection of the Jewish people with Palestine" and granted them the right to reconstitute their national home in that country. Britain was to facilitate immigration and encourage settlement of Jews on the land; Hebrew as well as English and Arabic was to be an official language, and a Jewish Agency—an organization which would later become of great importance—was to cooperate with and assist the British in building the home.

Even before the Palestine Mandate was confirmed by the League Council, the Arabs rioted in protest against the increasing inflow of Zionists from abroad. In 1929 a murderous outbreak against the Jewish population took place, inspired by Haj Amin el Husseini, the Grand Mufti of Jerusalem, who was the spiritual and political leader of all the Arabs in Palestine.

In the mid-1930s the persecution of the Jews of Germany, Austria and Czechoslovakia, and the unwillingness of still underpopulated Western Hemisphere countries and Australia to open their doors to those who were fleeing for their lives from central Europe, made many Jews turn to Palestine for sanctuary. The Arabs reacted with a full-scale revolt that began in the spring of 1936. The riots occurred first in Jaffa, then wherever there were Arabs and Jews in the same place. The list of dead mounted and life in the towns was disrupted by an Arab general strike. The British rushed in military units from Egypt, Malta and England, and finally restored order.

IT was in these years that British policy toward the Jewish people hardened. Confronted by Adolf Hitler's alarming rise in Germany and fearful that a great war was imminent, Britain began making extraordinary attempts to befriend the Arab nations, whose lands sheltered so many British economic interests (especially oil) and military bases (especially around the Suez Canal). In 1939 the British issued a White Paper, technically called Command 6019, providing that only 15,000 Jewish immigrants would be admitted to Palestine each year for five years, and after that no more at all, unless the Arabs approved. Thus the Jews would be forced to remain forever a minority. Also, they would not be permitted to buy land except in certain limited areas. And the British government would do everything in its power to enable an independent Arab Palestine to come into being. Instead of assisting the Jews to settle in the land, as the League of Nations had directed, Britain would now keep them away.

The Jews were understandably bitter. As Ben-Gurion (then head of the Jewish Agency) stated after the Nazi invasion of Poland, "We shall fight the White Paper as if there were no war and the war as if there were no White Paper."

During the early 1940s, while some Palestinian Jews were being trained by the British to parachute into Nazi-held Europe and organize underground resistance, others were trying to outwit the British by smuggling Jewish refugees into Palestine from Jewish ships. The anti-British guerrilla activity was carried on by three underground organizations. The Haganah (defense) had been founded in the 1920s by the Jewish community of Palestine for purposes of defense. Haganah members had to smuggle weapons into the country, or buy them surreptitiously from British soldiers. Training took place in schools and hospitals. An alarm system warned of the approach of the British.

Smaller in membership than the Haganah but intensely active was the Irgun (Irgun Zvai Leumi or National Military Organization), an outright terrorist group of several thousand fighters and active sympathizers who provided the necessary funds and permitted their homes to be used as hiding places. The Irgun was an offshoot of the Revisionist party, which advocated a state that would include the land of Transjordan. The third organization, called the Israel Freedom Fighters and popularly known as the Stern Gang, made up an extremist section of the Irgun that split off in 1941. Under its leader Avraham Stern, this small band specialized in outright assassination. Stern was caught by the British and shot, but his group continued to operate.

WHEN the war in Europe ended, all elements in Palestine began to consolidate their positions for what was to become the final struggle. The Arab states, by declaring war on Germany when the defeat of the Axis was certain, had become allies of the western powers, and under British prompting they formed the Arab League, which warned against any compromise on Jewish immigration. In September 1945, the U.S. began taking a direct hand in the situation, and President Truman requested the British to admit 100,000 refugees to Palestine. This the new Labour government—pro-Zionist before it came to power—refused to do.

With so many refugees languishing in camps in Europe, Palestine's Jews were infuriated by the British decision, and terrorist activities were stepped up. In June of 1946, Haganah forces attacked British communications and dynamited bridges. The British retaliated with mass arrests. Even leaders of the Jewish Agency—the organization that had originally been set up to assist the British in building a national home for the Jews—were taken from their homes and imprisoned. In July, Irgun blew up a wing of the King David Hotel in Jerusalem containing British offices, with the loss of nearly a hundred British, Arab and Jewish lives. The British commanding general issued an insulting order forbidding fraternization with Jews in order to "punish Jews in a way the race dislikes more than any other, by striking at their pockets and showing contempt for them." Matters had now reached a point beyond calm consideration.

Upon request of the British, the United Nations General Assembly met in Special Session in the spring of 1947. An 11-man Special Committee was appointed, the 19th to visit the land since the establishment of the Mandate. The Committee's majority report called for the partition of Palestine into an Arab state, a Jewish state and an internationally administered Jerusalem, the three parts to be linked in an economic union. The British, still siding with the Arabs in order to protect their own interests, strongly opposed such a partition. The United States voted for the majority report. Late in the evening of November 29, 1947, the Assembly approved partition, 33 to 13. Ten countries, including the United Kingdom, abstained. The Assembly requested Britain to leave Palestine within eight months.

THE Jews of Palestine celebrated wildly when the news was received. In eight months their long-awaited state would come into being. It had been a costly wait. Only now was the outside world beginning to get all the details of the extermination of the six million Jews in Europe. Although the Nazis' gas chambers and crematoria were being demolished, there were still refugee camps full of Jews who had no place to go. But now, once the U.N. resolution was implemented, there would finally be a place for them.

Many Arabs, however, took the action as a signal for the worst outbreaks of lawlessness modern Palestine had ever known. The next few months were called "an experiment in anarchism." In most cases the British—who could easily have maintained order—merely watched as Arab bands roamed the countryside committing murder, arson and robbery, attacking convoys en route to Jewish settlements and killing drivers and passengers. Haganah men found with weapons were arrested by the British, while the Arabs were able to receive shipments of arms from abroad that had been sent across the unguarded frontiers.

HAIFA'S 70,000 Arabs and 80,000 Jews carried on sporadic warfare for four months. Then the Haganah, in order to make the city secure as a communications center, launched an attack against Arab strong points, and an all-night battle took place. The next day Arab and Jewish leaders met to sign a truce and to discuss a way of allowing the Arabs to stay in Haifa. But it was too late: an order had arrived from the Grand Mufti directing them to leave.

Haganah sound trucks went out, urging the Arabs to remain, but in the end all but a few thousand of them fled. They were in the vanguard of the Arab refugees who today, with their children, number in the hundreds of thousands. The refugees' plight in their camps just over the Israeli borders constitutes a major and continuing international problem.

Violence was common. From Transjordan the British-trained Arab Legion prepared to march. More and more British arms were flowing into Egypt. One morning British soldiers drove three truckloads of dynamite into one of Jerusalem's principal streets of shops and flats and set it off, injuring and killing 175 Jews who had been sleeping. Meanwhile, the British Treasury blocked all Palestine bank accounts. Weeks before they were to leave, British communications workers dismantled part of the cable and wireless system.

In this supercharged atmosphere, the terrorist Irgun went wild. Trucks trying to reach

Jerusalem from Tel Aviv with food and medicine were being shot up by Arab villagers along the route, and the Irgun took it upon itself to be responsible for wiping out such opposition in the Arab community of Dir Yassin. Before the Jewish terrorists left the village, 254 Arab men, women and children had been brutally killed. Ben-Gurion angrily waved aside the Irgun explanation, and the text of a Jewish Agency statement expressing horror and disgust was cabled to King Abdullah of Transjordan. The Irgun also made an unauthorized attack on the Arabs of Jaffa, who thereupon joined the growing ranks of refugees.

THE top command of the Jewish Agency had in effect been a shadow government all this time, ready to take over with Ben-Gurion as leader as soon as the state was declared. But few men in history had ever had to face all at one time as many problems as Ben-Gurion did in the weeks preceding the departure of the British. He had expected that the British would turn over to him at least the skeleton of the government they had built in their 30 years in Palestine, but it now became apparent that hardly a law book, calendar pad or other accouterment of government would be left. Some files that would have helped in organizing a new government were burned.

There were indications that all the Arab neighbors were preparing to attack. The Haganah was ill-prepared to fight a war. Its few planes had a cruising speed of only 80 miles an hour. There were hardly any shells for the few available mortars. It had fewer than 200 heavy machine guns. Jerusalem was completely cut off now from the rest of Jewish Palestine and was short of food, water, fuel, ammunition and medicine. Seventy-seven doctors, nurses and professors on their way to the Hadassah Hospital and Hebrew University on Mount Scopus were waylaid by Arab irregulars, and while British troops in the vicinity maintained a hands-off policy the Arabs killed all 77.

The British had announced that they would not follow the timetable laid down by the U.N.

but would leave at midnight on May 14. Ben-Gurion issued a statement that the moment they did leave a Jewish state would be declared. But May 14 would be a Friday. At sunset the Jewish Sabbath would commence and for 24 hours no religious Jew would be able to sign his name or travel in an automobile. If the ceremony were to begin at 4 p.m., however, it would be over before the sun had officially set. Secret invitations were therefore delivered by hand to 200 important Palestinian Jews to be in Tel Aviv's Municipal Museum at 4 p.m. sharp on May 14 in "festive dark clothes." The time and place were to be kept strictly confidential.

On Wednesday of that week, members of the shadow government met and argued over whether the country should be called Judea, Zion, Eretz Israel (Land of Israel) or something else. Ben-Gurion suggested "Israel." A vote was taken, and the proposal carried.

The ceremony on Friday began with the Israel Philharmonic Orchestra playing the Zionist song "Hatikvah" (The Hope), which would be the Israeli national anthem. Then Ben-Gurion began to read the text of the independence proclamation.

The document—just 979 words—traced in sharp, clear sentences the life of the Jews from the dawn of their history to that moment. Israel was to be a state based on liberty, justice and peace; it would cooperate with the United Nations and uphold the principles of its charter. The holy places of Christians and Moslems would be safeguarded. The nation would strive for peace with the Arabs.

IT took Ben-Gurion 17 minutes to read the document. Then he announced the state's first decrees: the British White Paper (Command 6019) was annulled. So were other ordinances that had restricted Jewish immigration and purchase of land. Otherwise, until a new legal code could be devised, the law in force under the British Mandate would remain valid.

At 5:25 a.m. the next day, while Ben-Gurion was making a broadcast to America, the new state had its first air raid, an Egyptian bombing of Tel Aviv. Later that balmy Sabbath armed contingents from Egypt, Lebanon, Syria, Transjordan and Iraq joined in a concerted attack on Israel. They were later assisted by Yemenite and Saudi Arabian troops.

At a press conference in Cairo, Azzam Pasha, Secretary-General of the Arab League, declared: "This will be a war of extermination and a momentous massacre which will be spoken of like the Mongolian massacres and the Crusades." After 27 days of fighting, Count Folke Bernadotte of Sweden, the United Nations mediator, arranged a ceasefire. Both sides wanted a breathing spell, the Israelis because they were almost out of supplies and ammunition, the Arabs because they wanted to take stock of what had happened. The Arabs had been halted almost everywhere, and the Jewish forces had succeeded in keeping open a road to Jerusalem.

In early July the fighting began again. The Israelis captured Lydda airport and the Arab towns of Ramla and Nazareth. Planes that had been smuggled out of the United States and across the Atlantic by young American, Canadian and South African pilots, many of them non-Jewish, bombed Cairo and Damascus. Improvised Israeli gunboats shelled the Lebanese fishing port of Tyre. A corridor to Jerusalem was secured. After 10 days of Israeli victories, both sides agreed to a second truce.

TWO months later Count Bernadotte finished work on a plan to bring peace to the Middle East by severely reducing the Israeli territory. One afternoon while the Swedish mediator was on his way to a conference in Jerusalem, his car was waylaid by four terrorists, who killed him and one of his aides. His plan died with him. Ben-Gurion's cabinet offered a $20,000 reward for the capture of the assassins, but they were never apprehended.

Bernadotte was succeeded as U.N. mediator by Ralph Bunche, the American diplomat who had been his assistant. Bunche was a patient and tactful negotiator; furthermore, the time was ripe for a settlement because Egypt had suffered heavy casualties and its supply lines

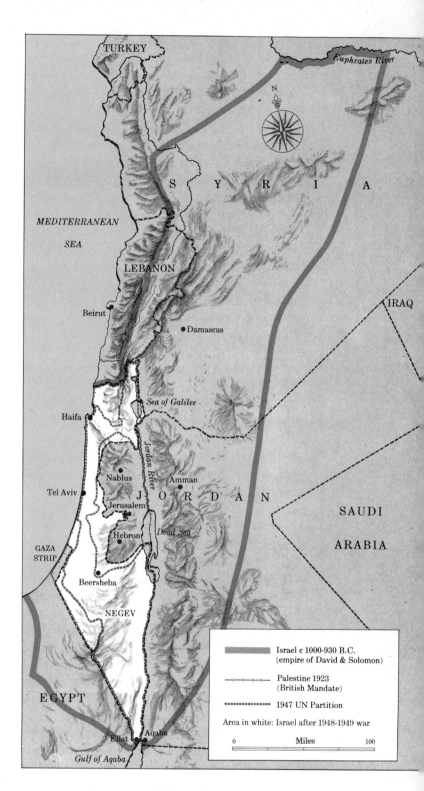

Israel c 1000-930 B.C.
(empire of David & Solomon)

Palestine 1923
(British Mandate)

1947 UN Partition

Area in white: Israel after 1948-1949 war

0   Miles   100

ISRAEL'S BOUNDARIES in Biblical times and after the 1948-1949 war of independence are shown above. Areas won in that war enlarged the new state. Under David and Solomon the kingdom had reached its greatest extent.

were overextended. An armistice agreement between Egypt and Israel was signed on the Greek island of Rhodes on February 24, 1949. Jordan, Lebanon and Syria signed later; Iraq, Saudi Arabia and Yemen never did sign.

Israel now settled down to the vital task of making a nation. The first election to fill the 120 seats in a unicameral parliament, or Knesset, was contested by 21 parties. Ben-Gurion's party, Mapai, won 46 seats, three times as many as Herut, the political successor of the Irgun. The first Knesset included three Arabs and 11 women. Chaim Weizmann, who had fought Zionism's battles abroad most of his life, arrived in Israel in triumph and was elected the country's first president. As titular head of state he asked Ben-Gurion, the chief of the largest party, to form a government.

THE Negev—the huge desert area in the south—had been awarded to Israel under the U.N. Partition Plan of 1947, but 15,000 Egyptian troops still held parts of it, including the ancient cities of Gaza and Beersheba. An Egyptian truce violation gave Israeli forces an excuse for Operation Ten Plagues, an attack which liberated Beersheba and put all the Egyptians to rout except 2,500 who were completely surrounded in several small villages in the north of the Negev. As it happened, one of the officers in what was known as the Faluja Pocket was a young Egyptian captain named Gamal Abdel Nasser—later Egypt's president—who conferred with the Israeli officers during negotiations that led to the final withdrawal of the surrounded soldiers and their return to Egypt.

The early days of the state were difficult. There was not enough food, and the country was living from ship to mouth. There was no housing for the immigrants who were pouring in. The Arab nations had instituted an economic boycott of Israel. Israel could survive only if generous Jews in the rest of the world, especially in the U.S., continued to give financial help. One story of the early 1950s was of a man who approached Ben-Gurion for a job and was told he could be Colonial Secretary.

"But we don't have any colonies yet, do we?" he asked.

"No," Ben-Gurion replied, "and we don't have any money, either, but we have a Minister of Finance." Despite this outward insouciance, the need was desperate, and world-wide Jewry responded magnificently. In the first 13 years $1.5 billion poured into Israel.

Another problem with international implications was Jerusalem, which the U.N. had said was to be an international city. The fighting had ended with the Arab Legion holding the Old City, which contained religious shrines of all three religions (Judaism, Christianity and Islam), and which Jordan promptly annexed. The Israelis held the New City, and this they quickly incorporated into their state. There was strong objection among foreign governments to the abrupt rejection of the idea of international rule. Within Ben-Gurion's Mapai party there was argument over how quickly Jerusalem should be made the actual working capital of Israel. A compromise was finally worked out whereby some branches of the government, including the Foreign Ministry and the Knesset, continued to be housed in Tel Aviv, while other departments moved to the Biblical city. Later the Knesset and all the ministries except that of Defense went to Jerusalem.

THE greatest internal crisis in the years that immediately followed independence was caused by the government's decision to demand and accept reparations from Germany. The government's position was: "Let not the murderers of our people also be their inheritors"—in other words, the people of Germany should not be allowed to keep what they had taken from the Jews.

While the Knesset debated, crowds of people objecting to any dealings with the Germans rioted in the streets of Jerusalem, automobiles were overturned and burned, 13 policemen were wounded in the fighting and then some of the mob attacked the Knesset. But eventually the reparations agreement with West Germany was signed, and $822 million worth of machinery, ships, rolling stock and raw materials soon began to move to Israel. Some Israelis never forgave Ben-Gurion, and when railroad trains arrived from Germany as part of the reparations they took a vow never to ride in them.

Toward the end of 1953, Ben-Gurion submitted his resignation and moved with his wife to an austere desert settlement, Sde Boker (Field of the Cattleman), in the heart of the Negev. He was anxious to "catch up with my reading," and he also wanted to try to inspire the youth of Israel to leave the cities and become pioneers. After more than a year of leading a simple life, writing essays, shearing sheep and standing watch against Arab infiltrators, he was persuaded to return to the government. In 1955 he again became Prime Minister.

WHILE the country's internal structure crystallized, external pressure built anew. Led by Egyptian President Nasser, the Arab nations, which had steadfastly refused to recognize Israel or to sign any sort of peace treaty, prepared for war. From the Gaza Strip, an Egyptian-held area jutting into Israel, countless raids were launched on civilian targets. Egypt also closed the Gulf of Aqaba to Israeli ships by refusing them passage through the Straits of Tiran and thereby making impossible any real development of Israel's commercial gateway to the south and east. Late in October 1956, Egypt, Jordan and Syria signed an agreement placing their three armies under Nasser's command. In reply, Israel on October 29 began an air, sea and land operation against Egypt. Britain and France, both vexed at Nasser's recent seizure of the Suez Canal Company, soon joined the attack. Their sudden participation brought about a world crisis.

On the eighth day of the war, Israeli commanders reported that the Egyptian garrison guarding the Straits of Tiran had surrendered. The occupation of the entire Sinai Peninsula had been completed. A thousand Egyptians had been killed and almost 6,000 taken captive. Israeli losses were 181 dead and one prisoner. France and Britain had acceded almost immediately to the U.N. demand for a ceasefire and withdrawal. But it was not until the following March—after the U.N. had called six times on Israel to withdraw from all occupied territory, and the U.S. had promised to help keep the Gulf of Aqaba open—that the last Israeli soldiers finally returned to their homes.

Eleven years later, while the other nations of the world watched with feelings compounded of guilt, awe and *déjà vu*, events repeated themselves. This time the stakes were higher and Israel, on its side, played the game alone. In the decade intervening, Egypt, aided and abetted by the Soviet Union, which was making a strong bid for Arab support, had rebuilt its military machine. Once more the bickering Arab countries closed ranks and began to mobilize. Terrorist attacks across the Israeli border were stepped up. On May 18, Egypt demanded and obtained the withdrawal of the U.N. peacekeeping teams that since the 1956 truce had been stationed in the Gaza Strip and the Sinai. With the U.N. gone, Nasser's next step was to blockade the Straits of Tiran once again.

IT may well be that Nasser, in order to recoup his declining prestige in the Arab world, was playing at brinkmanship; but if so he overplayed his hand. On June 5, 1967, in stunning predawn air strikes into neighboring Arab lands, Israeli jets all but eliminated Arab air power—and with it any chance of an Arab victory. Once more Israeli armored columns streaked across the Sinai, this time reaching the Suez Canal and the Straits of Tiran in just three days. Along Israel's eastern border, the Jordanians were pushed out of Jerusalem and back across the Jordan River, while the Syrians were driven almost to the gates of Damascus. The entire operation, a classic that will be studied for years by military strategists, had taken two days less than it had in 1956. This time, however, Israel declined to return to the indefensible boundaries of 1949, or to agree to trust its future security to the dubious capacity of the U.N. to keep the peace. The Arab-Israeli confrontation had entered a new phase.

Founder of modern political Zionism, Theodor Herzl sits with crossed arms between his mother and Jewish author Israel Zangwill

A Hardened Will to Create a State

Zionism, the triumphant movement to create a Jewish homeland, was not led by wild-eyed zealots. It won out largely because its followers worked astutely in a wide variety of fields. Some were unofficial diplomats in the capitals

amid other delegates to the Sixth Zionist Congress in 1903.

of Europe. Others were tireless fund-raisers and publicists. Thousands bravely set out for the farming frontiers of Palestine. In 1948, when Israel was born, this tough-minded idealism gave it the strength to survive its bloody birth.

BRITISH ALLY of Zionism, Lord Balfour (*left*) attends the dedication of Hebrew University in 1925 with Sir Herbert Samuel (in cap and gown); Judah Magnes, the university's chancellor; and Chaim Weizmann (*right*), who obtained British support for a Jewish homeland.

U.S. ZIONISTS prominent during the 1920s (*below*) include (*left to right*) philanthropist Nathan Straus, U.S. Supreme Court Justice Louis D. Brandeis and Rabbi Stephen S. Wise. The numerous Zionist groups in the U.S. raised millions of dollars to buy land in Palestine.

ISRAELI STATEHOOD was boldly proclaimed in 1948 in the face of chaotic civil

IN TEL AVIV only hours after the British departure, David Ben-Gurion announces that Israel is a state. The next day the U.S. gave the nation de facto recognition.

IN JERUSALEM buildings stand gutted on Ben Yehuda Street after anti-Jewish terrorists blew them up in February 1948. The Palestine Arabs hoped to drive the Jews out of the country before it could be partitioned by the U.N. The British, although still in control, made little effort to stop the raids and counter raids, and on May 14 they evacuated Palestine, leaving it in a state of riot-ridden anarchy. Fighting continued for eight months, until the Arabs finally agreed to an armistice in 1949.

49

SWIFT, BLOODY WAR erupted in 1967, and for the third time in 19 years Israel humiliated the Arabs

THREE BURNED MIGS, caught on the ground at an air base near Cairo *(above)*, are evidence of the knockout blow with which Israel destroyed the Egyptian air force.

JEWISH INFANTRY (*above*) moves forward along a bitterly contested ridge just inside Syria. During the 30-hour battle, Israelis claim, the Syrians lost 2,000 men.

TWISTED ARMOR lines the road at Mitlas Pass in the Sinai (*left*) where Egyptian units stood to face the on-rushing Israeli tanks, only to be devastated from the air.

ISRAELI COMMANDOS fight their way into the Old City of Jerusalem through St. Stephen's Gate (*right*). It took Israeli forces three days to secure the entire city.

VICTORY'S SPOILS *were many, but true and lasting peace remained elusive*

THE WAILING WALL *(above)*, symbol of Jewish hope made inaccessible by partitioning of Jerusalem in 1948, is visited by ex-Premier Ben-Gurion *(right, in light hat)*.

NARROW STRAIT, the entrance to the Gulf of Aqaba, is traversed by an Israeli freighter as Jewish soldiers who secured the Arab-held passageway watch from the shore.

THE SUEZ CANAL *(above)*, marking the end of the Israeli army's lightning dash across the Sinai Peninsula, is guarded by soldiers who are dug in on its eastern bank.

INSIDE THE WALLS of the Old City of Jerusalem, Jews and Arabs mix freely *(below)*, having evolved a tight-lipped modus vivendi following the war's uneasy truce.

WARILY HOPEFUL, European Jews sail for Israel, leaving their harrowing wartime experiences behind them. Mass immigration, spurred by the government, has more than tripled Israel's Jewish population since 1948.

4

The

Ingathering

of the Exiles

"THE State of Israel will be open to the immigration of Jews from all countries of their dispersion." Those words in the Israeli Proclamation of Independence, read by Prime Minister David Ben-Gurion on May 14, 1948, flung wide the gates. Two years later the Knesset approved the Law of the Return, which made it clear that the ingathering of the exiles would be hindered by virtually no legal barriers. Almost any Jew could enter Israel on the simple statement of his Jewishness.

Israel asked no questions about political beliefs, education or wealth. Under the Law of the Return it was—and remains—theoretically possible for an anarchist, unable to write his own name, with no trade or profession and without even enough money to buy a package of cigarettes, to obtain admittance to Israel.

Since the 1880s small groups of Jews had been settling in Palestine. Most of them were dedicated Zionists from eastern Europe. But the moment the state of Israel was formed, Jews started coming from everywhere—especially, at first, from war-sick Europe. Some of these immigrants were the survivors of the German concentration camps. Others were veterans of the partisan bands, men and women who had fought in resistance movements. Seventy-five thousand people arrived straight from the displaced persons camps of Germany, Austria and Italy. Among the early arrivals were 50,000 refugees who had been on illegal immigration ships that were intercepted by a British destroyer patrol before independence. They had escaped from concentration camps in Europe, only to be taken back to Europe or kept for years in British detention camps on Cyprus. In 1948 no one turned them back.

Israel was at war with the Arabs, Tel Aviv was being bombed and Jerusalem was cut off, but immigration continued. Food was scarce, the newcomers had to live at first in tent camps and flimsy shacks, and everyone seemed to be speaking a different language. Inevitably, there was wild confusion. A count later showed that nearly 500 refugees arrived daily—averaging out to one every three minutes around the clock. In the first seven months of independence a hundred thousand were admitted, almost as many as the British had permitted to enter during the 1940-1948 period. In the first 18 months some 340,000 came.

Czechoslovakia permitted 20,000 of its surviving Jews to depart. More than a third of Turkey's 80,000 Jews arrived by various routes. Some 36,000 arrived from Bulgaria. More than half of the remaining Jews of Yugoslavia took passage for Israel, as did all but a handful of Libya's. Jews came also from Poland, Romania, Hungary, Iran and China. Eventually more than 100 countries were represented.

SOME arrived so ill that they had to be immediately transferred from the ships and planes to hospitals. Few brought with them more than a single suitcase, or a small assortment of personal items tied in a bundle carried on the shoulder. Only four out of every 100 had any cash. Few could speak Hebrew. Many were doctors, lawyers, professors, clerks, shopkeepers—even though, of course, what Israel needed then were farmers, factory workers and managers, soldiers, pilots and laborers.

For some, the journey was a bewildering experience. Among the most perplexed were those who came by an airlift known as Operation Magic Carpet. In Yemen, the mountainous, primitive Arab country at the tip of the Arabian Peninsula, lived some 55,000 members of the oldest Jewish community in the world. Their legends told them that they were descendants of men and women who fled when Jerusalem was destroyed by the Babylonian king Nebuchadnezzar in 586 B.C. For 2,500 years, cut off from the rest of their people, the Yemenite Jews had kept their Jewishness alive. They could sing the Psalms in ancient Hebrew and in Aramaic, two of the languages of the Holy Land at the time of Jesus. From the 10th Century they had been considered the property of the local Moslem ruler.

THE Yemenite Jews lived in stinking ghettos, and as serfs they were forbidden to ride animals, to build houses higher than the lowest Moslem houses or to raise their voices in the ancient prayers. Eight of every 10 children born to a Yemenite Jew died in infancy. Intensely devout and with a deep knowledge of Biblical teaching, the Yemenite Jews were—and are—simple, honest, gentle people with olive skins and dark soft eyes. They are capable of delicate craftsmanship. Yet the conditions under which they lived were feudal and barbarous.

When news of Israel's independence reached them, they were hesitant about leaving Yemen. But when the proposed method of transportation on Operation Magic Carpet was mentioned, these gentle people who had never seen an automobile recalled the words of Isaiah: "They that wait upon the Lord . . . shall mount up with wings as eagles. . . ." Unafraid, the Yemenites crowded aboard DC4s, more than 130 to a plane, and clutching about them their sacred scrolls and prayer shawls, flew to Israel on the eagles' wings. Magic Carpet was not the only airlift. Another, entitled Operation Ali Baba, flew in a thousand Jews a day from Baghdad, until practically all of Iraq's 135,000 were in Israel.

On the day in 1948 when Israel was proclaimed an independent nation, some 655,000

Jews lived in the country—a few more than the number of men that the Bible declares Moses led out of Egypt. Before three years had passed, these 655,000 had taken in an additional 655,000 Jews from abroad; Israel's population had doubled. By 1965, 2.2 million Jews were living in Israel. In the middle 1960s, immigration dropped sharply—a fact which, combined with the low birthrate for the Jewish population compared to that of the Arabs in Israel, is a cause of serious concern to the planners of Israel's future.

There were, of course, displaced children as well as adults among the immigrants. Youth Aliyah, a lifesaving organization developed by a Baltimore-born humanitarian named Henrietta Szold, rescued tens of thousands of orphans from the streets and D.P. camps of Europe even before the state was created. After independence it continued to establish children's villages in which youngsters were taught a new way of life. Orphans from Yemen, for example, were persuaded to sleep in beds instead of under them; Cochin Indian children were taught that the use of soap was not dangerous. Fear was gradually eradicated from the hearts and minds of orphans from such diverse and unfamiliar places as Samarkand in the Soviet Union and Marrakech in Morocco.

THE ingathering was not achieved without stresses and strains, heartaches and bitter disappointments. During those early years if there was not enough to eat or the water supply stopped functioning or the electric power failed—or even if a waiter spilled the soup—the Israelis would half-facetiously blame the occurrence on the ingathering of the exiles. A stock comment in those days was: "For two thousand years we Jews have been hoping and fighting and praying for the Return—and it had to happen to me!"

Prime Minister David Ben-Gurion and his government were confronted with problems as difficult as those they had faced immediately before independence. In the confusion, many mistakes were made, but most Israelis put up with rationing and paid higher taxes with only a nominal amount of grumbling. Many of them took on two or three jobs simultaneously, took pride in what was being accomplished and made wry jokes about themselves.

"How do you say hello in Hebrew?" a newcomer asked an oldtime Israeli.

"Shalom," said the other, using the word which translates literally as "peace."

"How do you say goodbye?"

"Shalom."

"Then how do you know whether you mean hello or goodbye?"

"That's just the trouble, we don't know whether we're coming or going!"

It took shrewd planning to handle 1.2 million immigrants in the short span of 16 years—the high tide of immigration—and the cost was staggering. The Jewish Agency, the organization that had played such a vital role in the drive for independence, managed and financed the transportation of the immigrants to Israel. The Agency in turn was supported by money raised among Jews abroad, particularly by the annual drives in the United States of the United Jewish Appeal, which has raised the phenomenal sum of more than a billion and a half dollars for Israel. Even that amount was far from enough to cover the outlay. Permanent housing and the training of the immigrants in new skills, which would enable them to play useful roles in the economy of the country, were financed by the Israelis themselves. As additional immigrants arrived, the Israelis were forced to increase their own taxes and for a long period to live at an austerity level.

WHILE the immigrants were being assembled in transit camps abroad, a Jewish Agency staff in Israel organized kitchens, nurseries, kindergartens, first-aid stations and other vital services. Tents were pitched, often in frantic haste. All over the country, camps, hostels and temporary dwellings sprang up. Old British army camps were used as makeshift hospitals. Thousands of mud huts, abandoned by the Arabs during the brief 1948 war, were taken over and made semihabitable. Jaffa, almost deserted by the Arabs during the war, was filled with Jews from 50 or 60 countries. So were Acre, Ramla and other former Arab communities.

Then came the era of the *ma'barot,* or transit villages, consisting of rows of huts, tents and packing-box lean-tos, which sprang up on the edges of Israeli cities and large towns. Some of the immigrants housed in these villages came in time to earn their own livings, but many became discontented and disillusioned shanty-dwellers. By the end of 1951 the population of the transit villages had been augmented by the 100,000 Iraqi Jews who had arrived almost destitute because the Iraqi government had seized all their property.

THE run-down *ma'barot* villages were an understandable source of embarrassment to the Israelis. As rapidly as possible more permanent housing was built. Eventually a "ship-to-settlement" scheme was devised. While immigrants were still en route to Israel they were interviewed and classified, then sent straight from the docks to assigned places in established settlements. Nearly 150,000 immigrants from North Africa were satisfactorily settled under this plan. The collective settlements known as *kibbutzim* absorbed thousands of other immigrants.

All the agencies involved in immigration and resettlement tried to make the newcomers self-sufficient as soon as possible, but grumbling was common in the post-independence days. One favorite story concerned a woman who arose from the audience at the close of a government official's lecture and said: "I have a family of 12. We came here four years ago with nothing. We are still living in crowded, temporary housing. You say the state has done things for all of us. What's it done for me?"

"What are your children doing?" the speaker asked.

"Three are in school."

"And the rest?"

"Two are in kindergarten, two are in the army, two are already married, one is studying

at a trade school and two others have jobs."

"And your husband?"

"He works in the post office."

There was a roar of laughter.

In the late 1950s, when most of the immigrants were coming from North Africa, fears were often expressed that the "Orientals," as the Jews from African and Asian countries came to be called, would give Israel a character no different from those of neighboring states. "Sometimes, walking in the streets of Tel Aviv, you feel you're in the Casbah of Algiers," a well-traveled American visitor observed during the period. Between 1948 and 1963, 55.4 per cent of the immigrants had come from Asia and Africa, and 44.6 per cent from Europe and America. Nevertheless there has been no perceptible alteration in the nation's western-oriented cultural character.

The "Orientals" were only one of the problems faced by Israel in creating a homogeneous state. It was—and it remains—an enormous task to effect a cultural and social merger between swarthy Kurdish Jews who wore the turbans and baggy trousers of the Middle East, Jews from Shanghai who had fled from Russia years before, nomadic Jews from Arabia whose wives scarred themselves for beauty's sake, English Jews with Oxford degrees and German Jews versed in medicine and philosophy.

THE mingling of cultures is reflected today in the most mundane areas. Clients of a restaurant in Galilee are handed a menu which lists among its offerings Russian borsch, Czech dumplings, Spanish omelet, North African salad and Polish stuffed fish. "What is North African salad?" a tourist once asked the waiter-proprietor. "Just lettuce and tomatoes with a little dressing," he said. "But I had to call it North African salad. The Moroccans complained that I didn't have any Oriental dishes on the menu."

The mixing has had interesting results. Many individuals became convinced, during the early years of statehood, that a new type of Jew was being created in the country—a different man physically, ideologically and even spiritually from his immediate forebears. "The greatest thing happening to Israel," former Prime Minister Ben-Gurion has said, "is not the buildings, the fields, or the plantations, but the way the people are being changed."

THE government has little if any choice of the ingredients going into the Israeli mixture. If a country in Africa or Europe still having a large number of Jews should force them to emigrate, the entire flavor of Israel might be changed, for the principle of the Jewish Agency, which remains in charge of such matters, is to bring Jews from the Diaspora to Israel whenever the opportunity offers. The Israeli government has not given up hope for an influx some day of immigrants from Russia, and it believes that a considerable number of the Soviet Union's 2.5 million Jews would leave for Israel if permitted to do so. While the Soviet Union in theory grants exit visas to its Jewish citizens who want to emigrate to Israel, in practice only a handful of old people with children in Israel have been able to leave the Soviet Union.

Obviously, too, if any considerable percentage of the 5.7 million Jews in the United States were to take up Israeli residence, the character of Israel would be considerably altered. As a matter of fact, Ben-Gurion has frequently displayed his annoyance that fewer than 10,000 American Jews have settled in Israel. He had hoped that there would be many—at least among the ideologically involved American Zionists—who would contribute their brains, skills and energies to Israel. He has suggested that a Zionist who does not emigrate to Israel cannot properly call himself a Zionist.

But even without a sizable North American spicing, there are enough ingredients to give piquancy to the ultimate concoction. It will take several generations to see what an actual mixing of the many diverse types will produce, but already there is a typical Israeli human product: the Sabra. "Sabra" is the Arabic word for the fruit of the cactus, tough and prickly on

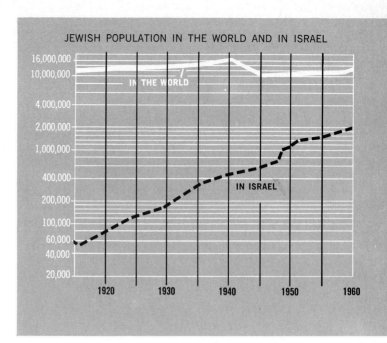

JEWISH POPULATION IN THE WORLD AND IN ISRAEL

IN THE WORLD

IN ISRAEL

POPULATION CHANGES in world Jewry and in Israel are shown on a logarithmic graph—one which is compressed toward the top to accommodate differing sets of figures.

the outside but sweet on the inside. The word is used figuratively to indicate anyone born in Israel.

Although generalizations about so large a group—more than 40 per cent of all Israelis are now Sabras—are difficult, some can be made. The most publicized type of Sabra is a handsome, healthy and tough-looking young man who seems to be a full head taller than his parents. He is self-reliant and forthright. He spends much of his time in movie houses and espresso bars, and talks knowledgeably about soccer, motor scooters and transistors. He tries to imitate American young men in his dress. He is quick of mind, although cynical. He has little understanding of anti-Semitism because he has never in his life encountered any manifestation of it. He scorns anything connected with what he calls "the ghetto mentality" of some of his elders.

Most Sabras are intensely proud of their culture and traditions, but consider themselves to be more Israeli than Jewish. Understandably, they want to be normal citizens of a normal country, and they are eager to get on with the job of creating a normal country. They take Israel and themselves very seriously. Preferring action to talk, the Sabras say: "Just tell us what to do and we'll do it our way."

Other Sabras enjoy books, concerts and lectures, have little interest in clothes, wear their shirts open at the neck and may not even own a necktie. They have a deep sense of loyalty to each other, tremendous energy and an apparently inexhaustible capacity for work. Many of them are more interested in science than in politics and want to acquire as much technical education as possible, in the belief that Israel's future lies as much in science and technology as in agricultural pioneering.

Rabbi Nelson Glueck, the American archaeologist, once explained why he always takes Sabras with him on his excavations in the Negev and elsewhere: "They're tough, rambunctious, terrifically hard-working. . . . They have a trace of the buccaneer and the adventurer about them. . . . They're the cock of the walk, but inside they're fabulous."

THE Sabra girls are fiercely independent creatures, neither asking for nor receiving any special consideration because of their sex. Part of this may be attributable to the fact that since the 1948 war, young women have been subject to compulsory military training and even to drilling in the use of firearms. In the army they grow accustomed to acting tough and being tough. They live in barracks separate from those of the men, but often eat, drill and make field trips with them.

On the negative side, Sabras can be characterized as provincial, brash, unbending and at times disrespectful. In the late 1950s, some Sabras took to playing a dangerous game. To fill the void of adventure created by quiet on the borders, Sabras in the army sometimes crossed the Jordan frontier to make a 16-mile trip behind enemy lines to visit the ruins of the ancient city of Petra. A few of them were caught and killed by the Jordanians. But those Sabras who managed to return alive from the Petra ruins were considered to be heroes by their friends.

There is some delinquency among the Sabras, most of it limited to petty thievery: stealing cars for joyrides; snatching windshield wipers, hub caps and car mirrors for sale; and taking fruits and vegetables from open-air market stalls. In 1965 there was sufficient juvenile delinquency to account for 30 per cent of the entire Israeli crime rate. Social workers and police attribute the high rate to a number of factors, including the breakdown of the old patriarchal family system and the waning of the "pioneering" spirit.

THE Sabras are only the most noticeable of a changing people. Israeli women have been granted many rights by the Knesset. Paradoxically the first Arab women in the world to win the right to vote were those of Israel. Women have complete equality with men before the civil law, including the right to hold property in their own names.

The man who has fought hardest for women's rights is Zalman Shazar, who became Israel's third President in 1963. While his office is largely ceremonial, he is the country's most respected citizen. Born in Russia, he immigrated to Israel in 1924, became editor of an influential labor daily in Tel Aviv, and active in Ben-Gurion's Mapai party. He wrote Israel's Declaration of Independence, became its first Minister of Education and fathered the compulsory education law.

Israel's Foreign Minister from 1956 to 1966 was Golda Meir, the first woman in the non-Communist world to hold such a position. A former Milwaukee schoolteacher who was born in Russia and who came to Israel from the U.S. in 1921, she is now secretary-general of the Israeli Labor party, Mapai. Four deputy speakers of the Knesset are women, and so are some of Israel's best musicians, painters, scientists and doctors. In a hundred ways, Israel is pioneering new freedom for women in the Middle East as it hastens about its task of creating a new people in a reborn land.

At Lydda airport a planeload of Moroccan Jews, carrying their belongings in shopping bags, enter their new land full of hope.

"Any Jew Who Wants to Come, May Come"

The bold avowal quoted at left, from an Israeli pamphlet on immigration, defines both the purpose and the strength of the new nation. At its beginning, the number of Jews who wanted to come was staggering—341,000 in the first 18 months, more than a million and a quarter within the first two decades. Today the DP camps in Europe are long since empty, but a new tide is flowing from a different quarter. Daily, refugees from Moslem North Africa arrive by plane. No longer is the problem of their absorption mainly physical—how to house, clothe and feed so many. Rather the question is how to integrate these new arrivals, whose culture differs so greatly from that of European Jews, into the existing national fabric.

TRANSFORMING immigrants into productive citizens is achieved through well-organized programs

A FAMILY from Algeria (*left*) arrives in a newly built frontier town. The box that the boy is carrying is filled with groceries supplied by the Jewish Agency for Israel.

A HEALTH NURSE (*right*) cares for an impoverished family that is living on relief. Many immigrants discover that they are simply not equipped to fend for themselves.

IMMIGRANT CHILDREN (*below*) attend school at Hazor, in Galilee. Their teacher has elected to fulfill her two-year military obligation to the state through educational work.

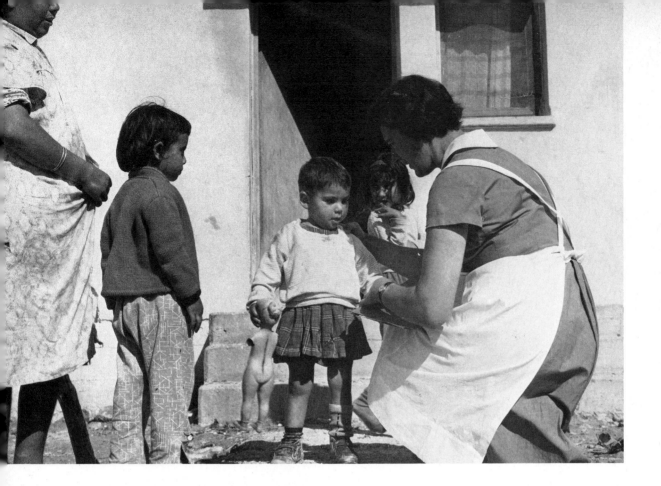

ADULTS LEARN HEBREW (*above*) at an intensive orientation course for professionals, like doctors, who face language examinations before being allowed to practice.

BOYS LEARN CARPENTRY in a village youth center. Although many of their fathers entered the country as unskilled laborers, these boys will not be so handicapped.

ASSIMILATION of newcomers is rapid, but there are still differences between the native and the immigrant

ON THE ROAD in Jerusalem (*left*), Sabras (native-born Israelis) race home from the Hebrew University campus.

IN TURKIC DRESS, Jews from Bukha- (*opposite*) play native instruments celebrate an Israeli national holida

AT A CELLAR CLUB, young Sabras (*below*) wear casual clothes and the careless air that now characterizes them.

*THE GREAT TIDE of immigration
is over, but thousands of settlers
continue to arrive annually,
reminding Israelis that their country
has not ceased to be a promised land*

JAMMING THE DECKS of a liner docking at Haifa, a shipload of newcomers await the moment when they will first touch Israeli soil.

GLIMPSING ZION for the first time, exultant shipboard arrivals get a view of Haifa buildings, patent proof that Israel is indeed a reality.

PATRIARCHAL LEADER, David Ben-Gurion dominated Israel's political scene in the critical years after independence. Although the main crisis has passed, he still thunders against those seeking luxury and city lights.

5

Establishing a Democratic System

THERE is nothing markedly different about the politico-legal system of Israel if its operations are compared with the practices and procedures of Britain, France or the United States. But it is always necessary to remember that Israel lies in the Middle East, on the edge of another world. The country is a solitary oasis of democracy, imported almost directly from the West, in a vast area of military dictatorships, feudalism, primitive concepts and non-western ways of thought and behavior.

But much of the raw material of Israeli democracy differs from that of western states. Visitors to a modern city like Tel Aviv, seeing movie theaters, luxury hotels, expensive dress-shops and swimming pools, are surprised if a waiter in a restaurant inserts his thumb in the soup he is serving. The darkness of his skin should tell them that he may be a North African who until just a few years ago had never seen a flush toilet, slept in a bed, eaten with a fork, had a tooth filled, been X-rayed or used a handkerchief, because he had lived all his life in a remote village in the Atlas mountains.

Similarly, an observer of western-style democracy in action in Israel may forget that many of those casting ballots in the last—or the next—election were recent arrivals from backward parts of Asia or Africa, and that for them voting is as strange an experience as saddling a camel would be for a New Yorker. Nevertheless, every man or woman over the age of 18, Jewish or not, is entitled to vote as soon as his name can be registered on the voting rolls of the state—and the registration process is swift and simple.

ASIDE from the necessity of integrating recent arrivals unfamiliar with democracy into the state, Israel's most vexing political difficulties arise out of proportional representation. Proportional representation, or P.R., is a voting system by which minor parties are enabled to obtain seats in the Knesset and representation in the Cabinet. In principle, P.R. is a highly democratic procedure which gives minority opinion a voice in government. But its opponents believe that the system contributes to instability in government and that it gives too much power to minor factions. During its first 19 years of independence, Israel had six national elections and a number of Cabinet crises, in part because of the maneuvers of the small parties. Former Prime Minister David Ben-Gurion has been among those who contend that the country cannot afford this disruption of normal life. As far back as the first political campaign in 1948, Ben-Gurion said jokingly to the American ambassador: "Please ask President Truman to share with us the secret of the American two-party system."

Under Israel's version of proportional representation the citizen votes not for a given candidate but for a party—and thus for its political philosophy and its election platform. Each party presents the voters with a list of candidates. The Knesset contains 120 seats because traditions say that more than 2,000 years ago the leadership of Israel was vested in a 120-member body known as the Knesset Gedola, or Great Assembly. The larger parties' lists therefore contain the names of 120 candidates. Smaller parties do not present that many.

If Party A polls 50 per cent of the total votes cast, it wins half the 120 seats, and so the top 60 persons on the party's list take office. If Party B polls one third of the total vote, then the first 40 men and women on its list are declared elected. If Party C gets 1.7 per cent of the total vote, it is entitled to just two seats. It is possible for a party with votes left over to give them to another party with which it has previously established a working agreement. For example, if Party C obtains 2 per cent of the total vote, or three tenths of 1 per cent more than is necessary for two seats, it has some votes left over which it can give away to a friendly rival in return for the rival's support for Party C programs. The rival party then adds Party C's votes to fill out its own percentage and perhaps gains an additional seat for itself.

THERE are other difficulties created by the proportional-representation system. After an election, the President of Israel, who is elected by the Knesset for a five-year term, calls on a member of the Knesset (by custom the leader of the party which has won the most seats) to form a government. In each of the first five elections, Mapai, the party headed by Ben-Gurion, polled the greatest number of votes, but never more than 38.2 per cent of the total. Therefore, each time Ben-Gurion was asked to head a government, he had to form a coalition of enough parties to give him working control of at least 51 per cent of the votes in the Knesset. This meant giving places in his Cabinet to members of minor parties, who are picked for the posts not by the Prime Minister but by the minor parties themselves.

In 1965, when 13 parties won seats in the Knesset, Levi Eshkol, Ben-Gurion's successor, faced a similar situation. The alignment of Mapai with Achdut Ha'avoda, a left-wing socialist party, won 45 seats—16 short of a majority. Eshkol then formed a coalition with the National Religious party (an Orthodox group), Mapam (a non-Communist Marxist party) and the Independent Liberals. The coalition was supported by various splinter groups and controlled 75 of the 120 seats.

Negotiations to establish the new governing coalition lasted a full two months. The demands that the smaller parties made upon Eshkol as their price for joining the coalition illustrate the power of these parties. Eshkol had to negotiate an agreement with the National Religious party, which demanded far more rigorous Sabbath laws. In the past, Achdut Ha'avoda has won support for one of its pet projects, increased civilian supervision of the armed forces.

DESPITE such anomalies in what is after all a secular state, although one in which religion is vastly important, it appears that proportional representation will remain. The smaller parties, aware that they would lose bargaining power if P.R. was abolished, have so far blocked efforts to change the system.

The innumerable parties which at one time or another have contested Israeli elections represent every shade of political and social thought. On the far left is the small but active Communist party. Anti-Zionist, it has obtained most of its votes in recent years from Israeli Arabs, particularly during the periods when President Nasser of Egypt has swung his weight in support of the policies of the Soviet Union. On the far right is the party known as Herut, whose name means "freedom." An outgrowth of the Irgun, the terrorist group of the years before independence (see Chapter 3), it calls for the re-establishment of the country's "historic" boundaries, which would mean incorporating the whole of the Arab state of Jordan into Israel. Herut also proposes the reduction of governmental controls over private enterprise. Between these extremes are Mapai, whose policies approximate those of the British Labour party; the religious parties; Mapam (United Workers' party); the Liberal party, which hopes to encourage free trade and private enterprise; and Rafi, Ben Gurion's splinter group that broke with Mapai in 1965.

With so many parties in the field, political argument in Israel is often intense and acrimonious. Election campaigns are nevertheless quite proper, and even staid. In an attempt to keep down extravagance and to obviate unfair advantage to large parties that have ample funds to spend, the law forbids the employment of films and entertainment to attract the public to political meetings. Electoral laws also prohibit the use of loud-speakers except to amplify speakers' voices at meetings, and they rule out distribution of gifts, food and drinks during a campaign. For a full month before the elections, candidates may not appear in newsreels. Each party is entitled to a total of 25 minutes on the state radio, plus four minutes for every seat it holds in the Knesset.

In each election thousands of ballots are cast by people who have never had the privilege of voting before, either because they had always been second-class citizens in countries like Iraq or because they came from countries like Yemen in which free elections are not held.

For years each party has employed a Hebrew letter as its symbol in all its printed appeals. On election day a voter going into the polling booth finds stacks of printed slips bearing the different party symbols. He takes the slip of his choice and seals it in an envelope, which he drops into a ballot box in the presence of the election committee. It is a simple system which helps to solve the problems encountered by newcomers not yet fluent in modern Hebrew.

DURING the years of independence, David Ben-Gurion has been by far the most important political figure in Israel. Intense and stocky, with a bristling halo of white hair, given to ringing pronouncements and Biblical quotations, he has been more than once likened to a patriarch out of the Old Testament. A man interested in matters of the mind, he has sometimes shocked the Orthodox by expressing an interest in—and familiarity with—non-Judaic religion. On a visit to Burma, he once spent nine days taking instruction in the philosophy of Buddhism. On occasion he likes to retire to Sde Boker, a settlement in the Negev, spending his days meditating and reading. He spent 15 months there from 1953 to

1955, and he returned to Sde Boker in 1963, when he again resigned as Prime Minister.

In or out of office, Ben-Gurion has had his share of political troubles, chief among them being "the Lavon affair." In 1954, while Pinhas Lavon, then a Ben-Gurion protégé and a potential successor to him as the leader of Mapai, was Minister of Defense, a security operation mounted by Israeli secret agents in Egypt somehow misfired. The complete details of the operation have never been revealed, but it is believed to have involved terrorist activity in Egypt, and the capture and execution of Israeli agents by Egypt. Lavon resigned as defense minister—or was forced to resign—under circumstances shrouded by secrecy, and, at Ben-Gurion's urging, subsequently became secretary-general of the Histadrut, the politically powerful Israeli labor federation.

IN 1960, Lavon asked Ben-Gurion to clear his name and thus smooth his return to the political arena. For a number of reasons, none of them entirely clear, the premier hesitated. There followed a most extraordinary, bitter and protracted political battle that enveloped the nation for the ensuing five years. The Lavon affair ultimately resulted in Lavon's complete political eclipse and Ben-Gurion's retirement from government.

When Ben-Gurion resigned in 1963 for "personal reasons" he chose as his successor the then finance minister, Levi Eshkol. Eshkol expressed a more lenient attitude toward Lavon, and even took steps that eventually cleared his name. Enraged, Ben-Gurion demanded a judicial review of the Lavon affair. This Eshkol refused, and with that the affair ended at last. But also ended was the Ben-Gurion–Eshkol friendship of many years. Opposed by his successor and by a majority of his party, Ben-Gurion bolted Mapai. He took his grievances and a number of young Mapai stars, such as Moshe Dayan, hero of the 1956 Sinai campaign, into a new party, called Rafi. In the November 1965 elections Rafi, organized too late and with too little, received only enough votes to send 10 members to the Knesset. Eshkol had clearly beaten his former mentor at the polls. From then on Ben-Gurion's political career was over and he entered the ranks of elder statesmen.

The man who now became undisputed leader of Israel had been born in the Ukraine in 1895 as Levi Shkolnik. In 1914 he emigrated to Palestine and Hebraized his name to Eshkol. Levi Eshkol rose quickly from being a farmhand to leadership in the Histadrut and later in the government. An expert on land settlement and water distribution, Eshkol made his mark as Israel's second finance minister during the period when Israel was absorbing massive waves of immigrants. By the time Ben-Gurion called on him to assume power, Eshkol had already won a big following in the Mapai party for his ability to bridge opposing views and to arrange compromises. As premier he continues to be a peace-maker, a man who rules by consensus.

Following the 1965 elections, Eshkol faced a deterioration of security along Israel's borders, and an economic crisis at home. An increase in raids by Arab terrorists, particularly in Galilee, pointed toward an eventual confrontation with the Arab states. During 1966 and 1967 immigration fell off. Construction, one of the nation's largest industries, was severely cut back. Unemployment rose steeply and Israel for the first time in its history instituted the dole. The brain-drain became a serious problem as some of Israel's young scientists and engineers left for lucrative and more challenging work abroad. By the beginning of 1967 public morale was low.

IRONICALLY, it was on Israel's independence day in 1967 that word arrived of Egypt's massing of troops. In a fast series of head-swirling events the crisis intensified. The United Nations peace-keeping troops left overnight. The Straits of Tiran were closed. Jordan joined Egypt in a united military command. At the beginning of June 1967, Eshkol expanded his Cabinet to include nearly all factions in the Knesset, bringing in as defense minister Rafi's Moshe Dayan. The nation braced itself.

The war acted on Israel like a shot of adrenaline. In the euphoria that followed victory, Eshkol pressed ahead with plans to fuse Mapai with several other labor parties. His ambition was to build a political base broad enough to guarantee himself a freer hand in governing the nation.

DEMOCRACY in Israel has also had to face unique judicial problems. A lawyer or a judge must have a great deal of special knowledge, for the law as it exists today is as heterogeneous and conglomerate as the population of the country. First, there are the statutes put on the books since 1948. Then there is the code of British law taken over on the day that the British left and Israel was created. But those laws were not purely British, for the Mandatory power had performed a trick the Israelis were later to imitate: when the British inherited Palestine from the Ottoman empire after World War I, they took over the Ottoman Code in its entirety, later adding laws of their own making to it. Furthermore the Ottoman Code was not pure either. It was based largely on the Mejelle, a codification of Moslem civil law which included some French statutes. For lawyers and judges the Israeli legal system is thus a fascinating tangle, with endless opportunity for precedent and argument.

Strange legal situations have inevitably developed. In ancient Jewish law there was no prohibition against the taking of more than one wife. Starting about a thousand years ago, Jews of central and eastern European origin outlawed polygamy. But a few Jews from other areas remain polygamous to this day. The result was that when the new state of Israel passed a law against multiple marriage, some citizens felt that a blow had been struck at their personal liberty. The Israeli Moslems were particularly bitter, since Moslems may have as many as four wives. The complaint was taken to the High Court of Justice, which declined to interfere on the ground that the Islamic religion permits polygamy but does not demand it—that an Arab can be monogamous and still be a good Moslem. Thus, the court said in effect, the law

was not a restriction upon the practice of the Moslem religion.

There are still other holdovers from the past which complicate the Israeli judicial system. The Ottoman empire assigned certain "personal status" matters—for example, marriage, divorce, adoption, guardianship and legacies—to the jurisdiction of the religious groups that it governed. Neither the British nor the Israelis saw fit to alter the system to any major degree. Under Israeli law, a citizen must belong to a religious "community." There are a number of such communities, including Jewish, Moslem, Druse, Roman Catholic and others. Today, each community holds exclusive jurisdiction only over matters of marriage and divorce. Other personal-status cases can be handled either by the courts of the religious communities or by civil courts. But the net effect is that civil marriage and divorce do not exist in Israel. A citizen who wishes to make a legal marriage or to obtain a divorce outside the regulations of his community must leave the country to do so.

SINCE the religious parties are able to swing considerable political weight, it is not likely that the religious courts will soon—or ever—be abolished, even if the bulk of the voters wished them to be.

Despite all these anomalies and anachronisms, the Israeli legal system is efficient and just. Free legal aid is available to any accused person unable to afford a lawyer. All cases are heard in open court, except those involving minors, military matters or abnormal sexual crimes. There is no jury system. One, three or five judges hear a case.

Israeli judicial procedure attracted worldwide attention during the trial in 1961 of ex-Lieutenant Colonel Adolf Eichmann, the former Nazi Gestapo officer abducted by Israeli agents in Argentina in 1960 and brought back to Israel to stand trial on charges of complicity in the murder of millions of Jews in the Nazi crematoriums. Perhaps 50 per cent of Israel's population had had members of their families or close friends among the six million Jews put to death by the Nazis. Yet outside observers agreed that the District Court in Jerusalem gave Eichmann a fair trial.

After Eichmann was sentenced to be executed, he was given the scarlet prison garb of a man condemned to die. It was a custom borrowed from the days of the British, but the act encountered violent objections from a strange source—former members of the Irgun terrorist group, who remembered all too vividly that years before the British had given some of their own leaders just such costumes to wear before execution. The onetime terrorists were able to win their point; Eichmann was given an ordinary prison costume.

UNLIKE many young nations, Israel does not face threats to its democracy from its armed forces. In fact, the Israel Defense Forces —as the combined defense establishment of army, navy and air is known—is one of the strongest bulwarks of the democratic system. A descendant of the Haganah, the underground army which played so vital a role in the drive for independence, the Defense Forces is much more than a standard military establishment. It is also a grade school, a high school, a college and a university. For years it has been conscripting young men for 26 months and young women for 20 months (Israel is the only country in the world with peacetime conscription for women). Often the Defense Forces takes young people almost directly from the immigrant ships. If necessary, it teaches them to read and write Hebrew. It also gives courses in the Bible, the history of Israel, geography and mathematics. It teaches them decent table manners, how to brush their teeth, how to get along with people. It takes them on tours of the country, and gives them lectures on biology, astronomy, geology. It teaches them a trade so that when they finish their military service they will be able to become useful citizens immediately.

Under the general jurisdiction of the Defense Forces are other groups. One is the organization known as Gadna, from its Hebrew name, *Gdudei Noar,* or "youth battalion." It gives physical training and some grounding in military matters to youths between the ages of 14 and 18. Another is Nahal (*Noar Halutzi Lochem,* or "Pioneering Fighting Youth"), which 18-year-olds may elect to join for part of their two-and-a-half-year period of service. Nahal combines agricultural and military training in areas considered too dangerous or difficult for normal civilian colonization. On the Syrian border, for example, where the farms extend within pistol range of unfriendly neighbors, it is considered wise to have agricultural workers as skilled in the use of firearms and defensive natural cover as in the driving of tractors. Nahal tries to encourage its trainees to remain as farmers in these areas after release from service.

Despite all its nonmilitary activities, the Israeli army remains a superb fighting force. In normal times there are only some 50,000 men and women on active duty. In an emergency, however, the army can summon some 250,-000 personnel to duty within 48 hours. General S.L.A. Marshall, the American military historian, has noted that the Israeli reserve about equals the total reserve of the United States, except for the National Guard.

OF Israel's Sinai campaign against Egypt in 1956, Marshall added: "The performance . . . was always consistent with the maxim of Marshal Foch—Always audacity. In all ranks, it was risk, risk, risk." Former Major General and later Defense Minister Moshe Dayan likes to tell a story of that campaign which illustrates the principle. During the action a group of Israeli pilots was sent out to land at a certain remote spot and cut Egyptian telephone lines. The cutting device the men had been given proved ineffective, but rather than return to their base for a proper tool, the Israeli commander climbed into his plane and flew at full speed toward the wires, his landing gear up and his whirling propellers yards off the ground. The blades sheared through the wires as if they were pieces of cotton. It was a daredevil operation that might have cost him his life, but it worked.

Levi Eshkol, who became Prime Minister in 1963 after David Ben-Gurion's resignation, addresses a Zionist congress in Jerusalem.

The Crisis-Seasoned Government Elite

The men who fought to bring Israel into existence have continued to run its affairs. They are the nation's founding fathers as well as its politicians. Most of them came to Israel during the first decades of this century. Many were pioneer farmers, including a prime minister. Many were outstanding military men. But although they will someday be the heroes of Israeli schoolbooks, they have rarely been spared criticism by Israel's alert, politically sophisticated citizens.

MILITARY WIZARD, Defense Minister Moshe Dayan *(above, right)* visits the east bank of the Suez Canal in 1967 in the company of a team of U.N. observers.

MOMENTOUS EVENT, the formal dedication of the new Knesset Building in 1966 *(below)* is attended by representatives from 43 countries and a huge crowd of Israelis.

HEAD OF STATE, scholarly President Zalman Shazar rides through Jerusalem with his wife *(above)*. One of Israel's most beloved men, he fills a largely ceremonial post.

Shazar was elected by the Knesset in 1963 following the death of Israel's second president, Isaac Ben-Zvi. The new nation's first president was Dr. Chaim Weizmann.

SUAVE DIPLOMAT, Foreign Minister Abba Eban *(above)* directs a remark to an aide while attending a debate of the Middle East crisis at the U.N. in the summer of 1967.

AT WORK in downtown Tel Aviv *(above)*, where he represents the interests of British magnate Sir Isaac Wolfson, Herzog addresses an employee at his tourist office.

PLAYING HOST, Herzog entertains visiting actress Maureen O'Hara *(below)* and some friends at his home. Irish by birth (like Miss O'Hara), he came to Palestine in 1935.

KEY ADMINISTRATOR, Haim Herzog is one of many managers recruited from the ranks of the military

AS A MILITARY EXPERT, with the reserve rank of Brigadier General, he broadcasts to the nation in 1967. His wartime comments were later published in book form.

AT HOME with his wife Ora, Herzog plays with his daughter Ronit. Besides Ronit, the Herzogs have three sons; the eldest, Yoel, has served in the Israeli army.

IN THE GARDEN of his home in Zahala, a suburb of Tel Aviv, Herzog and his daughter Ronit look for a grapefruit that will be ripe enough to eat for breakfast.

BELATED JUSTICE came when
Adolf Eichmann, a notorious Nazi,
was tried in Israel in 1961

EVIDENCE ON ANTI-SEMITISM was meticulously accumulated at Jerusalem's Yad Vashem Institute (*above*), which undertook a detailed investigation of the Nazi era.

EVIDENCE ON EICHMANN, consulted by a worker at the institute (*above*), was part of the extensive documentary proof of Eichmann's deeds demanded by the judges.

DRAMATIC SETTING for the trial (*right*) included a bulletproof box for Eichmann, who was convicted of crimes against the Jewish people and humanity and was hanged.

NEW BUILDINGS rise along the Mediterranean coast as construction proceeds at the port of Ashdod. Since Biblical times little more than a sandy waste, Ashdod now handles the Negev desert's increasing mineral exports.

6

A Desert Brought to Bloom

TO the 1.2 million people who streamed in during the first 16 years of its nationhood, Israel seemed in many ways an inhospitable land. Those from Europe, accustomed to moderation in heat, wind and the other vagaries of nature, had great difficulty in acclimatizing themselves. The sun wilted them. The dry wind from the south, called by its Arabic name *khamsin,* blew sand into their eyes, ears and mouths, and depressed their spirits. In so small an area, contrasts were extreme. Temperatures in the Jordan Valley sometimes dropped to 20° F. in the winter and rose above 125° in the summer. In the nearby hill country, winter brought heavy hail, thunderstorms, high winds and occasional snow. In desert areas the annual rainfall often came to less than two inches. The newcomers found that in Israel the body needed to do a great deal of adjusting to get in tune with nature.

It appeared that there was little richness buried in the earth; neither gold, silver, platinum nor much uranium, iron or oil.

For centuries in Europe Jews had been denied the right to own fields and consequently had had little experience raising crops, but now, unless tens of thousands of the immigrants rapidly learned agricultural techniques,

Israel would be clearly incapable of building a healthy economy.

After agriculture the country needed industry. Yet in few of the lands to which they had been dispersed had Jews ever become skilled factory workers. It was not certain that doctors, lawyers, professors and storekeepers could be quickly converted into farm hands, truck drivers and factory workers.

Moreover, the land desperately needed to be defended against the Arabs. As recently as World War II, Jewish leaders had argued in one world capital after another for the right to organize an independent Jewish unit to help in the fight against Nazi Germany. The defeat of the Arabs in 1948 was proof enough that Jews could fight. But after that victory a modern army had to be financed, organized, equipped and trained.

THE Arab economic boycott against the Jews of Palestine was intensified with the establishment of the state of Israel. This meant that citizens of neighboring states might desperately need steel pipe, spare parts for a typewriter, surgical instruments or medicines that were being manufactured a few miles away across an invisible border line—but their governments would not permit them to buy from an Israeli. It meant that under pain of imprisonment they had to let foodstuffs rot rather than sell to an Israeli.

Israel was also the victim of a secondary boycott. The Arab Boycott Office of the Arab League warned foreign companies that anyone who engaged in even the slightest dealings with Israel would suffer economic sanctions. A French automobile company was told that unless it closed down its assembly plant in Israel, not another car bearing its trade-mark would ever be sold in an Arab country. A British airline was warned that if its planes stopped at Lydda airport in Israel, it would not be permitted to land on any Arab flying field. U.S. and other shipping lines were told that if one of their cargo vessels carried as much as a single crate of Israeli goods, even if the shipment

were picked up at some neutral port, no ship belonging to any of those lines would ever again be permitted to call at any port in the Arab world. While most of these threats proved ineffective, the state's economic development was somewhat hindered.

Before the partition of Palestine the economy of the land had been based on the interdependence of Middle Eastern countries. In Haifa there were refineries that had operated 24 hours a day cracking crude oil brought in by pipeline from nearby Iraq. But during the 1948 war, the Arabs had cut the pipeline and the refineries had been forced to shut down. Where the oil to reopen the refineries and supply the future fuel needs of the new nation would come from, no one knew.

But quickly the land began to be filled with a contagious spirit of creation. Double lines of eucalyptus trees were planted on each side of the major roads to give shade—and to camouflage the movement of troops. School children celebrated an ancient spring festival called the "New Year of the Trees" by planting trees. When presidents, prime ministers and other foreign dignitaries visited Jerusalem, they followed the custom of paying their respects to Theodor Herzl, founder of political Zionism, by visiting his tomb in the Judean hills and planting trees in their own names on the slopes of Mount Herzl. A do-it-yourself forestry project was devised especially for American tourists, who were sold seedlings to plant.

THE trees have brought depth and much-needed shadows to a sometimes stark landscape. Since the founding of the new state, the government and the Jewish National Fund have directed the planting of more than 75 million trees, including six million in the Forest of the Martyrs outside Jerusalem. These trees were planted in memory of the six million victims of Nazi extermination. Throughout the country trees are now being planted at the coincidental rate of six million a year. For most Israelis the trees hold deep significance. They are symbolic of the Wandering Jew who at last has his roots sunk deep into the soil of his land.

In other ways the landscape of Israel changed from day to day. On the outskirts of Jerusalem, once-barren hills, plateaus and valleys were before long heavily dotted with the substantial modern buildings of a university, a hospital and government ministries. Settlements were established on almost every hillside in the country. Factories were sprinkled across the landscape from Dan to Eilat.

ONE of the most back-straining jobs was to terrace hillsides from which almost all soil had been washed away. There was, in fact, a desperate shortage of arable land. More than half of the nation's 8,000-square-mile land area lies in the Negev badlands. Part of the remaining acreage is covered with hills, mountains and sandy stretches that in 1948 looked worthless. It was a moot question how much was worth trying to reclaim; whether it was economically sound to try; whether a farmer could make a good living on any of it.

Before 1948 a great deal of farming by Jews in Palestine was performed by members of *kibbutzim*, or collective settlements. The first kibbutz (the word rhymes with "puts") was founded in 1909 on malaria-infested marshland near the Sea of Galilee by a group of immigrants from eastern Europe seeking to create a community based on the principles of utopian socialism. The land had been purchased from absentee Persian owners who referred to it as the "Death Spot" because of the great toll of life it had already taken. Known today as Degania (the name is derived from the Hebrew *daganit*, or "small blue cornflower"), the settlement is the showpiece of the kibbutz movement, with attractive and substantial homes and communal buildings, blooming orchards, citrus groves and flower beds. There are more than 225 kibbutzim scattered around the country, housing about 80,000 people.

The kibbutz way of life is communal. There are rigid qualifications for joining, but members may leave at any time. All members are on an even footing regardless of their jobs. Each member—physician or farm hand, teacher or cook—receives the same food, the same living quarters, the same social services, the same educational opportunities for his children. No one living in a kibbutz owns any private property, aside from small personal possessions, and no money circulates within the settlement. If a talented kibbutznik—a member of a kibbutz—wants to study art, he applies to the executive committee of the kibbutz, a group elected by democratic vote of all the members. If the committee thinks there are sufficient funds available, he is granted a leave of absence and given money to pay for the course. Members with special talents often obtain leaves of absence from the executive committee; many governmental posts and seats in the Knesset are held by kibbutzniks.

All major decisions taken by the executive committee of the kibbutz are subject to the approval of all the members. A work committee assigns jobs. Meals are eaten in a communal dining room. The rearing of the children is entrusted to specially trained members in a "Children's Home," which in most kibbutzim is the most comfortable and expensive building in the settlement. Late each afternoon, when fathers and mothers return from their work, the children arrive for a daily two-hour visit. When the parents leave for dinner in the community dining hall, they return the children to their own sleeping quarters.

THE selfless idealism of the kibbutzniks made possible the establishment of dozens of farming settlements in forbidding areas in the early years. These kibbutzim bore the brunt of the Arab attacks, since most of them were located near frontiers. At Degania, men and women armed with rifles, machine guns and Molotov cocktails withstood Arab tanks.

Some of the early kibbutzniks found the collective system too rigorous and restrictive, but were still eager to live in societies based on mutual assistance, and so the *moshavim*, co-operative smallholders' settlements, got their start. In a moshav each member lives in his own house and farms his own piece of land, but he and his fellow members jointly purchase or rent heavy equipment and market produce. In the 1960s there were 360 or so moshavim with a total population of more than 124,000. There are also many privately owned, individually operated farms. Together, these various agricultural enterprises produce foodstuffs valued at some $480 million each year. It is still necessary for Israel to import some grains today, but the country exports as much as $75 million worth of citrus fruits a year.

Although the population of both the kibbutzim and the moshavim has continued to swell, the increase has not been as rapid as the increase in the general population. In the mid-1960s only 18 out of every 100 inhabitants of Israel lived on the land, as compared with 30 in the urban areas of Jerusalem, Haifa and Tel Aviv, and 52 in towns and townships. Even the kibbutzim are no longer entirely agricultural. Many of them have established factories and holiday resorts as a source of additional earnings, as a cushion against a depression in agricultural income and to provide employment for handicapped and elderly members.

ANOTHER approach to the reclamation of Israel's unworked land involved the use of water. Water—or, rather, the lack of it—has played a dominant role in the history of man in the Middle East, where bloody feuds have often been fought over water holes and riparian rights. The prophet Ezekiel spoke of a time when the Negev would be traversed by a great river that flowed down through the wilderness where "everything shall live whither the river cometh." The Jordan is a brook by comparison with the Mississippi, the Amazon or the Nile, but all irrigation experts who have studied Israel's water problems have conceived plans for utilizing the Jordan in some way. The Jordan Valley Authority plan drawn by Dr. Walter Lowdermilk, a U.S. soil conservationist, formed one of the bases for the master water plan which Israel in 1956 adopted after years of investigation. It calls for making use of every available

drop of water before it is lost to the Mediterranean or the Dead Sea. As part of the over-all plan, a 154-mile network of pipes, channels and tunnels began in 1964 to carry water from the Sea of Galilee to southern farms and towns. A new process for the conversion of salt water into fresh water, invented by an Israeli, is being used in the Eilat desalinization plant. Israel and the U.S. have discussed cooperating in building an atomic plant to provide power for desalinization. Plans call for it to begin operation early in the 1970s.

THERE are other aspects to the master water plan. Forty-two years before the creation of modern Israel, the Zionist organization made a survey of the possibilities of reclaiming the Hula Basin, the triangular valley in the northeast corner of Israel in which three streams merge to form the Jordan River. Part of the valley was then covered by a great marsh and a muddy lake. In 1934 a concession was obtained to undertake the Hula reclamation, but work did not actually start until 1950. It took another seven years to complete the project, but by the time it was finished it had added 15,000 acres of exceptionally fertile soil to Israel's land area.

What the West was to the United States in the mid-19th Century, the Negev was to Israel in the early 1960s. "Go south, young man!" was the advice given to Israeli youth seeking pioneering adventure. Those who went found the Negev a fearsome place, but one to excite the imagination. The desert's eroded cliffs and wrinkled valleys seemed to resemble those of the moon. Yet many of King David's subjects lived in the northern Negev. It was in the Negev, at Sodom, a town on the Dead Sea, that Lot's wife, unable to resist the temptation to look back, was turned to salt, according to the Biblical story. At the southern tip of the Negev were King Solomon's copper mines and smelters. Uzziah, one of the ancient kings of Judah, built a network of military roads crisscrossing the area and, the Bible reports, constructed "towers in the wilderness and hewed out many cisterns." Under later peoples—the Nabataeans and the Byzantines—the Negev flourished. In those days it was dotted with fortresses and farming communities.

In the fighting that followed the partition of Palestine in 1948, the Arab and Israeli armies bitterly contested the Negev. When the hostilities ended, Israel was in complete possession of the desert area it had been assigned under the partition plan. The Negev's principal inhabitants were 15,000 Bedouin tribesmen who kept constantly on the move. Guidebooks listed the population of Beersheba, the major town of the Negev, at 3,000, but the census—if there ever was one—must have been taken on market day when the Bedouins were in town to do a little camel trading and buy an ounce or two of tobacco before vanishing again in the desert heat and dust.

EVEN before partition, young Jewish pioneers had begun the attempt to master the Negev. As early as 1948 there were 27 desert villages in various stages of development. Because Arab marauders roamed the desert at will, each of these places necessarily was a fortress. Either the villagers defended themselves or bore the consequences, for the nearest possible assistance was generally hours away.

By 1966 the Bedouins of the Negev had gained the company of 250,000 Jewish Israelis. Eilat, Israel's outlet to the Indian Ocean, the Pacific and all the countries of the Orient, had grown to a town of 9,700. Beersheba, after dropping down to 1,500 following the flight of its Arab population during the Israeli-Arab war, had more than 65,200 inhabitants.

As it happened, the development of Eilat was hastened by Egypt's refusal to allow Israel to use the Suez Canal to ship goods to the Far East from the Mediterranean port of Haifa. Israel made several attempts in the 1950s to ship through the canal to avoid the long trip around Africa, but each time the ships and their cargoes were impounded. Israel's only alternative was to use Eilat, located on the gulf at the southern tip of the Negev. But the gulf (known to the

Arabs as Aqaba and to the Israelis as the Gulf of Eilat) was closed to Israeli shipping because Egyptian guns commanded the Straits of Tiran at the point where the gulf empties into the Red Sea. When Israeli forces pushed into the Sinai Peninsula in 1956, the Egyptian guns were silenced. During the following decade, while United Nations troops stood guard along the waterway to insure unfettered passage, the straits developed into a thriving commercial gateway. The departure of the U.N. troops, upon Egypt's request, was one of the causes of the war that raged briefly through the Sinai Peninsula in 1967. As an additional alternative to the Suez Canal, Israel is planning a 45-inch pipeline that will bring crude oil from Eilat to the Mediterranean port of Ashdod and from there by tanker to Europe.

In Eilat, while steamers are being loaded with Israeli exports, tourists skin dive and small boys hawk bottles containing layer upon layer of the colored sands of the Negev arranged in geometric patterns. Yet life in Eilat demands toughness. The sun is scorching, and the cost of living is high because everything that is consumed must be transported by truck and plane from northern Israel. The government, to encourage the growth of the town, excuses Eilatis who contract to remain at least five years from paying some income tax and permits them to buy refrigerators and air conditioners without paying the normal purchase tax.

MODERN Sodom, 110 miles to the north of Eilat, is today the lowest peopled spot on earth, 1,286 feet below sea level. About 500 men are engaged there in extracting potash and other minerals from the Dead Sea. There are extensive natural gas reserves in the vicinity of Sodom which are also being exploited. When they were discovered in 1957, the discovery gave rise to a theory about a Biblical mystery. It was suggested that the destruction of Sodom and its twin city of Gomorrah might have been brought about by the explosions of such gas. The exact location of neither Biblical city is known today, although it is believed that modern Sodom lies in the vicinity of the ancient site.

Agriculture in the Negev has made enormous strides also. Tomatoes, melons and spring potatoes are flown to Britain and Europe out of season and retail there for less, despite the high cost of their transportation, than competing fruit and vegetables grown in the British and European hothouses.

But the greatest hope for the economic future of Israel and the Negev lies in the ability of its young scientists to use nuclear-age methods to solve, boldly and brilliantly, the problems that for so long have kept the Middle East a backward part of the world.

When it was disclosed in 1960 that Israel was building a second nuclear reactor, to be located in the Negev, there was some international alarm over the possibility that Israel might be attempting to enter the atomic-weapons club. But Prime Minister Ben-Gurion declared that the reactor would be used to train Israeli scientists and technologists in the construction of an atomic power station. Methods of converting sunlight into electricity are also being investigated in the Negev.

A MOST important influence in the lives of Israelis is the unique organization known as the Histadrut. This is the General Federation of Labor, but in size and scope it is unlike any labor organization anywhere else in the world. Its membership, including wives (who are given full membership status), totals over one million persons. It represents almost 90 per cent of the country's wage earners and collects dues that range from 3 to 4.5 per cent of the wages of all these workers. Almost half of the total goes into a gigantic "Sick Fund," which operates nearly a thousand clinics scattered around the country and more than 200 hospitals, convalescent homes and mother-child welfare stations.

Established in 1920 when Palestine's economic outlook was bleak, the Histadrut had to play a role assumed by private capital in other countries. Today it owns daily newspapers, the

A WHITE-COLLAR PAY CHECK

Monthly salaries of typical Israelis are subject to a broad variety of benefits and deductions. All figures are given at the official exchange rate of 3.50 Israeli pounds to the dollar.

Salary

Basic salary	$232
Cost-of-living allowance, which rises with increased prices	79
Seniority (four years)	32
Family allowance (wife, three children)	11
Overtime	5
Allowance for professional literature	6
Bus allowance for traveling to work	3
Total gross:	**$368**

Deductions

Income tax	$67
National Insurance (social security)	3
Surtax for June 1967 war	6
Immigrant absorption forced loan	12
Pension fund	16
Union dues to the Histadrut, including family medical plan	10
Office gift fund	1
Donation to Red Shield Society	1
Vacation savings fund	1
Total deductions:	**$117**
Net salary:	**$251**

largest sports organization in the country, a building and construction company with more than 30,000 employees and an industrial holding company. It controls cooperatives for the marketing of farm produce. It operates adult education courses, vocational schools and a pension fund. The Histadrut is part owner of an irrigation company and a shipping line. Its varied enterprises account for 25 per cent of Israel's entire national income, including about 70 per cent of all agriculture, 50 per cent of all building and public works, and 17 per cent of all the country's industrial production. Prime Minister Levi Eshkol was one of the founders of the Histadrut and nearly all the members of Israeli Cabinets have been dues-paying members of the organization. Members of the Histadrut also occupy seats in the

Knesset and hold other governmental and private positions.

To appreciate the extent of the Histadrut's far-reaching domain, it is helpful to imagine what it would be like if the President of the United States were one of the founders of a 60-million-member AFL-CIO which owned and operated hundreds of large hospitals, as well as several of the largest corporations and newspapers in the country, in addition to a large book-publishing firm, a couple of industrial towns and many of the major buildings in the United States.

Every few years members of the Histadrut elect delegates to a convention, which then elects a council, which in turn elects an executive committee that directs the union's affairs. Most of the political parties which take part in the country's general elections also present slates of candidates for the Histadrut offices. While Mapai, the dominant political party in the nation, was not able to poll more than 38.2 per cent of the national vote in the country's first five general elections, it obtained better than a majority in the Histadrut elections. This connection between Mapai and the Histadrut of course assists in making the organization politically powerful. Frequently, the government and the Histadrut clash, but the big labor organization retains a strong voice in the country's affairs.

RIGHT-WING parties in Israel attack the Histadrut from one week to the next. They refer to the organization's massive headquarters building in Tel Aviv as "the Kremlin" because, they contend, the Histadrut virtually runs the country. Opponents maintain that the Histadrut is a state within a state and they constantly call in vain for its power to be broken. Yet in national elections the public consistently gives three to four times as many votes to parties supporting the Histadrut as it gives to the party which campaigns most vociferously against the federation.

There is considerable private enterprise in Israel, side by side with the activities of the Histadrut. Millions of dollars of investment capital arrive from abroad each year. The annual campaigns of Israel's Development Corporation are held in many countries and have sold more than $850 million worth of State of Israel bonds, most of them in the U.S. An Investment Center established by the Israeli government under a Law for the Encouragement of Capital Investment had approved investments of $715 million in 2,700 working enterprises by 1965.

IN the early days of the state, matches refused to light, shoes disintegrated and clothes wore out rapidly. Now Israeli factories turn out a wide variety of articles, mostly of good quality. They make everything from false teeth to high-grade cement, from fishing nets to sports cars. Such exports totaled more than $400 million in 1966. Textiles, fashion goods, machinery, chemicals, pharmaceuticals and tires are among the largest earners of foreign currency for Israel. In the 1960s the country moved goods to Singapore, Teheran and Helsinki, and was actively selling in Africa and Eastern Europe.

Israel is also exporting locally produced radioactive isotopes for medical research, and submachine guns called the Uzi, after their designer Uzi Gal. In the late 1960s, more than $15 million worth of the Uzi guns had been sold to 30 countries. By 1962 Israel had become the second largest cut-diamond exporter in the world, with 203 firms importing raw diamonds from Africa, cutting and polishing them, and then sending them abroad. Almost a third of the diamonds go to the United States. In 1966, $165 million worth were exported from the country.

Israel is constantly searching to expand its foreign trade. Its exports to Africa and Asia are growing, and part of its success is due to the fact that it adapts its goods to specific local conditions. Tires that it exports to Ethiopia, for example, are specially developed for the stony roads in that country. As a developing nation itself, Israel has much to offer the underdeveloped world.

IN UNISON, children practice the recorder at a kibbutz, a kind of collective-farm settlement of Israeli origin.

The Struggle for a Margin of Comfort

Among the world's underdeveloped economies, that of Israel has run a unique course. Its development began not with efforts to move farmers off the land but with a drive to bring city people back to farming. The movement to establish kibbutzim, or communal villages, was only one of several back-to-the-land efforts, although its spartan ideals made it a perfect instrument for the needs of a pioneering society.

Today the pioneer pattern has itself begun to change. The kibbutzim have grown prosperous, but new settlers prefer a less communal life. Israel has also found it must develop industries to survive. Engineers, scientists and technicians are the newest pioneers in the drive to forge a modern economy out of limited means.

BY THE SEA OF GALILEE, young Israelis cultivate tomatoes. The workers are members of *Nahal*, an elite paramilitary corps specially trained to settle and defend frontline kibbutzim.

AFTER DINNER, with the day's work behind them, members of a prosperous kibbutz gather over *espresso* coffee in their recreation hall to discuss politics, gossip and play games.

THE STEADY REFINEMENT of living conditions has turned ragged rural outposts into well-run communities enjoying many town amenities

CO-OPERATIVE VILLAGE of Nahalal (*opposite*), an individualistic variant of the kibbutz called a *moshav ovdim*, has private farms encircling community-owned facilities.

PORTICOED SCHOOLHOUSE in the Kibbutz Yagur is a far cry from days when a shack, shared with another kibbutz, was all that could be given over for education.

CONCRETE-LINED CANAL, a part of the Jordan Water Project, carries fresh water from the Sea of Galilee to the parched Negev. Completed in 1964, the water project increases the country's supply by 84 billion gallons annually. But Israel still desperately needs more fresh water.

ARMED POLICEMAN guards a pumping station in Galilee, part of the mammoth Jordan project. Water in the artificial lake in the background is held in reserve in the event of a breakdown somewhere in the 150-mile-long network of pumping stations, canals, tunnels and pipelines.

WATER, one of the nation's pressing needs, is being systematically controlled to bring new land under the plow

PRECIOUS SWIRL of water is brought by an irrigation canal to a vegetable field bordering barren hills in Galilee (*right*). By means of careful draining and channeling, Israel has succeeded in tripling its supply of usable water.

NEGEV SUNFLOWERS, grown for their seeds and oil (*below*), blossom in village fields well watered by sprinklers. Without obtaining some form of artificial irrigation, hundreds of rural settlements would be unable to survive.

95

COPPER REFINERY in the desolate Negev processes ore from deposits unworked since King Solomon's time. Most of the copper is earmarked for Western Europe.

DEAD SEA SALTS are dug up in chunks from the bottom of an evaporation pond. They are turned into potash, used in Israel's growing fertilizer and glass industries.

A SHARP TRANSFORMATION has been wrought on the land's age-worn face

GEOMETRIC RANKS of apartment houses rise in the midst of wind-blown sand dunes near the coast seven miles below Tel Aviv. The apartment dwellers are suburban commuters, not agricultural pioneers. Since 1948 Israel has built more than 600,000 new housing units, many in regions that have not been inhabited since Biblical times.

Bathing in the Nile, the Pharaoh's daughter rescues Moses from the bulrushes, where he had been abandoned by his mother.

Choosing a king for Israel from among the sons of Jesse, the Hebrew prophet Samuel anoints David, the youngest of them.

ANCIENT PAINTINGS of Old Testament scenes are the world's oldest known Bible illustrations. Found in a Third Century Syrian synagogue, they were painted in spite of the Judaic law against depicting scriptural events.

7

The Fusing
of Faith
and the Arts

WHEN a boy in a European country or in America is given a Bible to read it is "religious instruction." In Israel he is studying not just the religion but the geography and literature of his country—as well as the faith of his fathers—when he reads, for example, the lament of King David over the deaths of Saul and Jonathan in battle against the Philistines at Mount Gilboa. Indeed, the boy's father may have had a flat tire driving through the Gilboan foothills the week before. In such homely ways does Israeli life intimately connect tradition and education. In turn, the arts of Israel reflect the nation's religion—a faith which affirms the importance of study and the intellect.

One evidence of the continuing importance of religion to Israel is the fact that the country contains 6,000 synagogues. Only a few—like that of the Hebrew University in Jerusalem—can be considered architecturally striking; the bulk of the synagogues are small and intimate. Others are merely rooms in private houses. All are well attended and serve not only as places of worship but as meeting places for entire communities. Jerusalem alone contains around 400 synagogues.

Within these thousands of places of worship there are considerable variations in devotional procedures. Broadly speaking, there are two major Judaic traditions: that of the Ashkenazim, or groups which originated in western, central and eastern Europe, and that of the Sephardim, who came primarily from Spain and other Mediterranean lands. There are also the so-called oriental traditions which are associated with Jews from the Middle East. All brought slightly differing rituals and observances of Judaic Law to Israel. In the West, especially in the United States, the Jewish religion is broken into three groupings: Orthodox, Conservative and Reform. Orthodox Jews believe in the strict observance of Judaic Law—613 different commandments are involved—as divinely revealed in the first five books of the Bible and as subsequently interpreted in later centuries by rabbinical authorities. These 613 commandments regulate literally every area of daily life, as well as birth, marriage, worship and death. Services are conducted almost entirely in Hebrew. Reform Judaism, a movement which began in Germany in the early 19th Century, is more liberal in its practices. For example, men and women sit together in Reform congregations, a practice forbidden by the Orthodox, and services and prayers are largely conducted in the language of the country in which they are being held. Conservative Judaism, founded some 40 years after Reform, occupies a position between these extremes.

IN Israel these differentiations have very little meaning. For the majority of the population, religion is identified with Orthodoxy, although there are half a dozen non-Orthodox congregations which have modified the ritual. In addition, there are Jews who say they are without religion. Something less than one per cent volunteered this information when the first census was taken in Israel in 1948. At the other extreme is the Naturei Karta (Guardians of the City), a sect of ultra-Orthodox Jews who refuse to recognize Israel's official institutions or representatives. Its members claim that the state came into being without the sanction of God. A special position in Israel is occupied by the Hassidim, another group within the Orthodox tradition. Some of the Hassidim immigrated to Palestine as early as the middle of the 19th Century. "In the land of Israel," one of their rabbis once said, "even the direction of a stick lying on the ground has holy significance."

Still other Jews in Israel, as elsewhere, look upon themselves as religious, but do not strictly adhere to traditional practices. In addition there are Jews—particularly among the young Sabras born in Israel—who are today seeking a new interpretation of life not necessarily within the Judaic tradition.

WITH all these variations, there is no more definitive answer in Israel than elsewhere to the question: What is a Jew? In 1958, when new identity cards were issued to the population, the government announced that anyone might identify himself as a Jew on his card who declared "in good faith" that he was a Jew and that he professed no other religion. Children, the government said, could be identified as Jews if both parents wished it. This meant, in effect, that even the child of a non-Jewish mother could be considered Jewish. The announcement caused considerable controversy in Israel. Orthodox Jews generally interpret the Talmud to mean that only the offspring of a Jewish mother can be a Jew. Two Orthodox members of the Cabinet resigned, and the Orthodox National Religious party introduced a motion of no-confidence in the country's parliament. The government won the motion, 60 to 41, but today, in practice, Israeli government departments use the religious definition as a rule of thumb.

Despite the overwhelming dominance of Orthodoxy, there is no national law regulating the public observance of the Sabbath and other religious holidays although a "Days of Rest Ordinance" lists Saturdays and the major holidays of the year (see Appendix) as "prescribed days of rest." Some local governments have passed municipal regulations for the purpose of keeping Jewish holidays holy. From sundown Friday to sundown Saturday no public buses may run, no movies may be shown and no shops may remain open in most cities and villages. Cafés are closed too, but restaurants may serve meals and a few pharmacies are permitted to stay open to sell medicines for emergencies. Buses are permitted to operate in the industrial seaport of Haifa. The service, owned by the bus-drivers' cooperative, was instituted before 1948, when the municipalities began to pass Sabbath ordinances.

In all Israeli cities crowds watch soccer on the Sabbath, but if a motorist drives through Mea Shearim, the section of Jerusalem where ultra-religious Jews live, his car may be spat upon or even stoned. No newspapers are published, but *Kol Israel*, the state radio, broadcasts through the day. The dial telephone system of course continues to function, although Orthodox Israelis neither make nor answer calls from sundown Friday until sundown Saturday. On the major religious holiday known as Yom Kippur, "The Day of Atonement," Israel virtually comes to a standstill. Yom Kippur is a fast day; no restaurants are open, and most of the populace attends all-day services in the synagogues. *Kol Israel* goes off the air and only emergency telegrams may be sent.

WHATEVER the Israeli's precise attitude toward his religion, the Bible is to him "The Book of Books." Interest in the Old Testament is intense throughout the nation. Each second Saturday night the President, Zalman Shazar, and some of the country's leading scholars spend hours discussing the Old Testament in the President's home in Jerusalem. The group is one of the scores of circles of the Israel Society for Bible Research.

During the celebration of Israel's 10th anniversary in 1958, the first of a series of international contests on knowledge of the Old Testament was held in Jerusalem. It drew contestants—many of them Christians—from 14 countries. The contender from Israel was one Amos Hacham, a 30-year-old, partially paralyzed clerk. The questions were sometimes factual and sometimes theological: "At the close of several books of the Bible, women are praised. Which books are they?" (Esther, Ruth, the Song of Solomon and Job.) "Where is the eternal nature of God's reign first expressed?" (Exodus 15:18—"The Lord shall reign for ever and ever.")

THE final round began at 8 o'clock on a summer evening in the outdoor amphitheater of the Hebrew University in Jerusalem. Every one of the 2,340 seats was taken, and many people were standing. Radio *Kol Israel* announced it would stay on the air until the winner was decided. Hundreds of thousands of Israelis sat around their radios hour after hour as Hacham piled up points. At 2 a.m. Hacham was proclaimed champion. The Judean hills echoed with applause. The tens of thousands of radios were shut off and a populace exhausted from excitement went to bed. Subsequent contests have attracted equally fervid interest.

Today, Israelis read newspapers in the language of the Bible. In the late 19th Century the ultra-religious residents of Jerusalem actually tried to prevent a zealous Lithuanian immigrant named Eliezer Ben-Yehuda from reviving ancient Hebrew and making it a spoken language again—on the grounds that it would be sacrilegious to use the holy tongue for mundane matters. Eliezer Ben-Yehuda was a newspaper editor who foresaw that when—and if—Jews returned to Palestine they would need a common language. He was to devote the rest of his life to resuscitating the language of the prophets. Hebrew had gradually ceased to be the major language in Palestine after the Jews of the 6th Century B.C. came under the domination of the empire of Babylon, whose language was Aramaic. The Hebrew that had come down through the centuries was for praying and for religious instruction; not for ordering groceries or giving directions to an office boy. The Hebrew Old Testament had a vocabulary of only 7,704 words. So Ben-Yehuda went to work searching in parchment manuscripts for the thousands of words that had been lost, or using Hebrew roots to create words that had not existed in the days of Abraham and Moses.

Ben-Yehuda spoke the language that he was reviving and insisted that his wife and children speak it. He tried to popularize it in his newspaper. Finally, he compiled a monumental dictionary listing tens of thousands of old and new words. Ben-Yehuda's eldest son, Ittamar Ben-Avi, reputedly became the first child in modern times to learn Hebrew as his native tongue, and an apocryphal story tells that his dedicated father kept him locked in the house for years in an effort to prevent him from hearing another language.

Gradually Ben-Yehuda won adherents. Eventually numbers of scholars were to continue his work. But matters moved slowly. At one point in Ben-Yehuda's campaign, two of his friends waited outside a school in Jerusalem for the children to come out, planning to knock the hat from the head of the first boy they saw. Their theory was that if he then reacted by crying *"Imma"* (mother), or some such word in Hebrew, it would prove that Hebrew had finally become the national language; if he shouted *"Mamale,"* the Yiddish equivalent, Ben-Yehuda had failed. What the boy shouted was *"Hamor!"*—the word which in both Hebrew and Yiddish means jackass. Yiddish, descended from German and containing many Hebrew words, is spoken by many Jews of European origin.

YET Ben-Yehuda's campaign finally succeeded. In 1920 the British High Commissioner, Sir Herbert Samuel, announced that Hebrew would be, with English and Arabic, one of the three official languages of Palestine. Modern Hebrew, now Israel's official tongue, has a vocabulary of almost 100,000 words—and even some slang. *Puntcher,* from the English "puncture," means anything that has gone wrong; *protectzia,* from "protection," means "pull" or "influence." Hundreds of thousands of Jews have learned the language since 1948. A daily and a weekly newspaper in simplified Hebrew are published for the newcomers. In order to help immigrants master the language quickly, the Ministry of Education and the Jewish Agency have organized intensive courses in Hebrew called *ulpanim.* More than 90,000 people have studied Hebrew in such courses, using modern teaching methods.

The teaching of language was not the only educational activity undertaken by the state in the immediate post-independence days. Within 16 months after independence the Knesset passed a sweeping compulsory education law—an action consistent with the traditional Jewish respect for learning but in dramatic contrast to the alarming state of the country's finances in the aftermath of the Arab war and the necessity of providing food and shelter for the increasing number of immigrants. The law provided that regular school attendance would be both free and compulsory for children aged five to 14.

THE law placed a staggering burden upon the state. Before independence all education was private, paid for by parents or civic organizations. The thousands of children enrolled under the new system required schoolrooms, books, chalk, paper, pencils and, above all else, thousands of teachers. At first almost any applicant was accepted for a teaching post. Cynics said that the only document needed by a prospective teacher was a birth certificate. The classes were held in tin huts, in canvas tents and in open fields, with the children sitting on planks placed across rocks.

Today Israel has the best elementary-school education system in the Middle East. It has a teacher now for every 23 pupils, compared with 48 in Turkey and 38 in Egypt; the ratio even surpasses that of Britain, which has one teacher for every 28 students. On the secondary-school level, however, education is neither compulsory nor free. The state and the municipalities give financial aid to qualified children whose parents cannot afford private-school costs.

Facilities for higher education have been steadily expanding in the years since statehood was achieved. But some institutions faced odd difficulties in their efforts to get going in the early days. During the 1948 Arab war, Israeli forces fighting Jordanian troops managed to hold part of Mt. Scopus in Jerusalem, where the Hebrew University had been located since 1925. As a result, when peace was established the university's buildings were isolated in an Israeli enclave surrounded by Jordanian territory. Under the terms of the U.N. armistice agreement which ended the war, Israel was entitled to free access to the enclave, but Jordan permitted only an armed convoy to pass through its territory every fortnight to relieve the police guards that Israel kept on duty. In the wake of the June 1967 war, Israel regained direct access to the university buildings.

In 1958, a newly constructed group of Hebrew University buildings was dedicated on the opposite side of Jerusalem. In them more than 12,000 students, including an increasing number of Americans, Africans and Asians, are enrolled. Fields of study include science, law, the liberal arts and Jewish studies. Tel Aviv has a smaller university which was opened in 1953. In Haifa is one of the best institutes of its kind in the world—the Israel Institute of Technology, known as the Technion. For engineers, architects, chemists and other specialists, the Technion is the Middle East's equivalent of the United States' top-ranking Massachusetts Institute of Technology. Still another university, Bar-Ilan, which specializes in religious studies, and general education, was dedicated in 1955 in Ramat-Gan, a town adjacent to Tel Aviv.

Scattered around the country are also kindergartens, nursing schools, agricultural and trade schools, teachers' colleges, and music and art schools. Even a hotel school has been opened which trains young Israelis to be good waiters in six months and chefs in 15.

Despite Israel's abiding interest in the traditions of the past, the country has a passionate concern for the contemporary arts. The grounds of many of the agricultural settlements are dotted with pieces of modern sculpture, the walls of homes and hotels are decorated with paintings by local artists, and the country abounds with good and bad practitioners in all the lively arts: playwrights, novelists, poets, sculptors, directors, producers, choreographers, dancers and musicians.

Throughout the nation, there are scores of amateur and professional musical groups—including everything from an opera company to chamber music societies to folk singers. The Israel Philharmonic Orchestra was founded in 1936. The orchestra's inaugural concert was given in a converted exhibition hall in Tel Aviv

THE HEBREW ALPHABET

Shown below are the letters of the Hebrew alphabet, with their equivalents in English. Letters can also indicate numbers. Only the letter "vav" represents a vowel sound. The other vowels can be indicated by special signs.

ALPHABET	NAME	TRANS-LITERATION	NUMBER
א	ALEF	-	1
ב	BET	B or V	2
ג	GIMEL	G	3
ד	DALET	D	4
ה	HAY	H	5
ו	VAV	V	6
ז	ZAYIN	Z	7
ח	KHET	Kh	8
ט	TET	T	9
י	YOD	I or Y	10
ך כ	KAF	Kh	20
ל	LAMED	L	30
ם מ	MEM	M	40
ן נ	NUN	N	50
ס	SAMEKH	S	60
ע	AYIN	-	70
ף פ	PAY	P or F	80
ץ צ	TSADE	Ts	90
ק	KUF	K	100
ר	RESH	R	200
ש	SHIN	Sh or S	300
ת	TAV	T or Th	400

with Arturo Toscanini conducting. The Philharmonic was the story of Israel in microcosm. Sixty of its original 72 musicians were European refugees. It has always operated with distinguished guest conductors and soloists, and it has toured North America, Europe and Asia. At home it gives 20 concerts a month, 10 months a year, even on nights when the hot *khamsin* wind almost suffocates audience and musicians alike, and the very thought of blowing a French horn is exhausting.

Serious drama is represented chiefly by three top repertory companies—Habimah, the Cameri and Ohel. Habimah, the first modern Hebrew theatrical company, was given the status of a national theater by the government on its 40th anniversary in 1958. In its years in the country it has produced plays by virtually every one of the world's major dramatists. Israel has approximately 300 actors and actresses earning their livelihoods in the theater, a high proportion for so small a nation.

The country is also producing literature out of proportion to its size. Popular books written and published locally can sell as many as 25,000 copies. Even a slim volume of Hebrew poetry will sell a thousand copies.

Among Israel's outstanding writers are the novelists S. Y. Agnon, who won the 1966 Nobel Prize for Literature, and Haim Hazaz, who has won numerous Israeli awards. Both writers have specialized in religious and folkloric subjects. Younger writers today, however, are breaking away from such traditional themes to concentrate on the contemporary problems of the country.

ART in the Holy Land received its first modern stimulus in 1906, when a Russian sculptor, Boris Schatz, founded an art school and museum in Jerusalem and called it Bezalel, after the craftsman who built the Biblical Tabernacle in the Wilderness. In the Bezalel school an attempt was made both to resurrect ancient crafts and to introduce fine arts in Palestine. For more than half a century the Bezalel National Museum has been a major influence on all

forms of Jewish art. On canvas many Israeli artists have expressed the reality of the Zionist dream in styles varying from primitive to abstract. Others have made successful attempts to pictorialize religious mysticism.

But Israeli painting today is little concerned with the past. There is a multiplicity of style, subject matter, media and treatment. Out of this may eventually come a typically Israeli art. Meanwhile, museums, galleries and art shops are full of the vigorous products of the striving.

There is plenty of additional artistic activity in the country. Israel has two flourishing art colonies. One is in Ein Hod, a village not far from Haifa. The other is in Safad, one of the northernmost towns of Israel. Its crooked lanes and alleys are lined with the homes of painters, sculptors and poets. Both colonies produce and exhibit sculpture and handicraft objects for sale, as well as paintings.

ARCHITECTURAL styles vary as much as those of the painters. There is "Early Tel Aviv," which even the most loyal Tel Avivians admit is bad—jerry-built, three-story apartment houses of cement and plaster, festooned with balconies, each one looking less attractive than the last. They contrast with the grain silo called Dagon on the waterfront of Haifa. The silo represents modern architecture at its most functional, with symbolic decoration identifying it with the ancient land of the Bible. Rising in the geographical center of Jerusalem is the Israel Museum, a complex of buildings dedicated to the arts. The complex includes the unusual "endless museum," a shrine built in the form of a cave to hold Israel's priceless collection of Dead Sea scrolls; the impressive Bronfman Archaeological Museum; and the Bezalel National Museum. Nearby is a majestic new Knesset building, with mosaics and tapestries designed by the artist Marc Chagall.

All these buildings have been constructed of the pinkish-streaked or yellow-white Jerusalem stone of which the landscape itself is largely made. A tourist is told a dozen times a day by guides and proud Jerusalem citizens that this was the one good thing the British did during the long years of their mandate: a British governor during the 1920s, Sir Ronald Storrs—who is famed for having figured prominently in the liberation of Middle East areas from the Turks in World War I—decreed that no structure could be erected in the New City unless it was built of the indigenous stone, which the Arab builders had been quarrying and using for centuries. The result is that Jerusalem, growing naturally from the hills that surround it, has a charm of its own.

DURING the early days of independence, in perhaps unconscious manifestation of the new freedom and in the interest of speed, the Israelis constructed a few new buildings in Jerusalem out of reinforced concrete, but then they returned to the use of the quarried stone. The one notable exception is the $30 million Hadassah-Hebrew University Medical Center, built on a plateau overlooking the ancient monastery village of Ein Kerem, birthplace of Saint John the Baptist. It replaces the old hospital building on Mt. Scopus, to which the Israelis were long denied normal access. This 600-bed institution—with an outpatient department that can care for 250,000 patients a year—seems to resemble at a distance some gigantic space machine. But in the opinion of architects, builders, doctors, nurses and hospital experts, it is a dream of planned efficiency. The medical school, staffed in large part by European refugees, has one of the finest faculties in the world.

The striking appearance of the combined hospital, medical school and nursing school is heightened by a dozen stained-glass windows, each almost 12 feet high, which symbolize the 12 tribes of Israel. The windows (see page 24) were designed by Marc Chagall for the Medical Center's synagogue.

Israel has an impressive health record. Almost all of the immigrants who arrived in the early years of independence were in poor physical condition. A large percentage of those who came from Africa and Asia had never had any medical or dental care. Some had incurable diseases, many had tuberculosis, most were undernourished. Among them were 50,000 victims of schistosomiasis, a disease of the tissues caused by parasitic organisms. There were thousands of cases of blood and eye diseases.

But by 1961 most of these diseases had been virtually wiped out. Before the state was created, Palestinian Arabs lived, on the average, to the age of 46. Within 10 years their life span had been increased to 61. The life expectancy of children at birth in the United States is 70 years, but in Israel, largely because of efficient and widespread public-health services, it is 72.1 years. In Egypt it is 52.7 years. The death rate—the number of deaths per 1,000 persons in a year—has dropped to 6.2 for Jews in Israel. For Arabs, it has been lowered to 6.4 as against 15.3 in Egypt. The infant mortality rate, generally considered by medical authorities a reliable index of the state of public health, rose to 52 per 1,000 in the days when the first rush of immigrants from Europe arrived, but has fallen steadily to 23.9 among Jews and 38.2 among non-Jews. In Egypt the comparable figure is 118.

SUCH achievements are a reflection of Israel's continuing interests in both medical and scientific research. The justly renowned center of research is the Weizmann Institute of Science, dedicated in 1949. It was an outgrowth of an earlier establishment founded by the country's first president, the late Chaim Weizmann. Situated in Rehovoth, a town near Tel Aviv whose name means "broad acres," the institute has related its interests to the land almost since establishment. Its first projects were investigations into the properties of fertilizers and the processes by which plants absorb minerals. Today the Weizmann Institute teaches in and explores such fields as applied mathematics, the production of isotopes for medical uses, the synthesis of proteins and the causes of cancer. A quotation from Weizmann is carved into Galilean marble on the campus. "I feel sure," it reads, "that science will bring to this land both peace and a renewal of its youth."

A Culture Cosmopolitan and Unformed

Despite the talents of Israel's artists and the keen appetite for culture shown by its citizens, Israel has not yet developed a uniquely Israeli art. The literature, painting and music produced today are cosmopolitan and varied, but for the most part they are produced by men born in Europe for an audience whose tastes were formed outside Israel. Such works do not of themselves add up to an Israeli culture. Only with the emergence of a new generation, steeped from birth in the distinctive atmosphere of the country, will there be an unmistakably Israeli stamp on the cultural achievements of the young nation.

UNDER DIMMED LIGHTS, Israel's 100-man Philharmonic Orchestra performs in the Mann Auditorium in Tel Aviv.

IN A ROMAN THEATER in Caesarea, the noted cellist Pablo Casals plays Bach. His accompanist: Rudolf Serkin.

EDUCATION is being adapted to meet the increased demand for technical skills

LANGUAGE SCHOOL for immigrants who have professional training offers intensive instruction in Hebrew to speed up the newcomers' incorporation into national life.

STUDENT GEOLOGISTS from Hebrew University (*left*), needed in the continuing search for new resources, gather around their professor during a field trip in Galilee.

TOWERING CYLINDERS of compressed gas are used for supersonic research at the Israel Institute of Technology, training center for engineers, architects and scientists.

LEADERS in the fields of art and intellect have been able to draw upon a rich variety of established cultural traditions

SELF-TAUGHT PAINTER, Shalom of Safed (*above*) executes Old Testament scenes in a naïve style. A watchmaker by trade, he took up painting at the age of 79.

CELEBRATED PHILOSOPHER, the late Martin Buber was one of the world's outstanding religious thinkers. His works have strongly influenced Christian theologians.

MYSTICAL SYMBOLIST, Mordekhai Ardon has exhibited his colorful compositions in the U.S. and Europe. Born in Poland, he received his art training in Germany.

In a Dead Sea cave a team of Israeli archaeologists sifts the earth for evidence of a Second Century Jewish rebellion. They uncovered

1,800-year-old military dispatches and skeletons of defeated rebels.

The Enduring Spell of Antiquity

WHAT professional bicycle racing means to the French, and mountain climbing to the Swiss, hunting for relics of the past means to Israelis, young and old. In a land where almost any archaeological discovery sheds light on the glorious past from which the Jewish people were cut off for so many centuries, it is no accident that everyone is fascinated by news of diggings. Many people become amateur devotees. Even tourists sometimes succumb.

Several years before the country's first golf course was opened at Caesarea, an Israeli tried to interest an American guest in visiting the ancient city by telling him of its historical importance. "You know, it was the capital of the Romans in Palestine for hundreds of years. You'll find it quite interesting." The visitor was not impressed, but his host continued. "King Herod the Great founded it about 22 B.C. and named it in honor of Augustus Caesar, and. . . ." The American finally made the trip reluctantly, but a few minutes after arriving in

Caesarea, he discovered three Roman coins in the sand. That did it. He promptly joined the ranks of those under the spell of antiquity.

Many prosaic pursuits in Israel take on a new dimension because of the chance that some treasure will be turned up. Bulldozers clearing the way for a new road have accidentally exposed the remains of villages buried for centuries. Men digging the foundations for a new apartment building have discovered antiquities that were worth more than the land itself. Arab school children playing in the ancient town of Acre have found many treasures, which are now housed in a former Turkish bath that has become the municipal museum.

ONE indication of the importance attached to archaeology in Israel is that even in the first years after independence, when taxes were being pushed higher and higher and every possible economy was being effected because funds were so urgently needed to care for the flood of new immigrants, archaeological activities were still given surprisingly generous official support. Another indication is that Israeli government publications list more than 60 archaeological museums and collections in the country.

At critical periods archaeology has helped solve grave military problems for modern Israel. The acting chief of staff at the time of the invasion of Israel in May 1948 was Yigael Yadin, the son of Professor E. L. Sukenik, a celebrated archaeologist. Following in his father's footsteps, Yadin had learned the terrain of Palestine by digging it up. When the Syrian army attacked, Yadin knew from his Biblical and archaeological studies that a similar invasion had taken place 2,800 years earlier, when the Syrian Aramaeans marched down from Damascus. In planning his defense, he took into consideration the theory that because the terrain had not changed, the Israelis' modern enemy would use the same route. He deployed his men accordingly, and the Syrians were as unsuccessful as before.

Later that year, archaeology came to Israel's aid again. The war with the Arabs was almost over, and Operation Ayin was designed to wipe out remaining Egyptian resistance in the Negev. The only usable road from Beersheba to the Sinai frontier swung in a wide arc and was heavily patrolled by the enemy. Happily for the Israelis, the operation was under the command of Yadin, then chief of operations of the Israeli general staff. "At my headquarters," Yadin recalls, "we had . . . a map of Roman Palestine and there we noticed an ancient road which led between Gaza and Beersheba. We asked the Southern Command to see whether this road was good and one of the scouts . . . called back and said: 'Difficult but possible.' He exaggerated the 'possible' since two-thirds of the road was covered by terrible sand dunes. So we planned to cover the dunes with Bailey bridges and, almost under the noses of the Egyptians, we forged ahead. Our column marched through the rear and caught the enemy. . . ." Several weeks later Egypt asked for an armistice.

ARCHAEOLOGY has increased the country's material riches. At first it was assumed that the earth held little if any mineral wealth. But Dr. Nelson Glueck, the learned rabbi who is president of Hebrew Union College-Jewish Institute of Religion and who is an eminent archaeologist as well, found himself puzzled by the reference in Deuteronomy 8:9 to the Promised Land as ". . . a land whose stones are iron, and out of whose hills thou mayest dig brass. . . ." Dr. Glueck was certain that "brass" was a translator's error for "copper." But no copper or iron had yet been discovered in the Holy Land. Further sleuthing led Dr. Glueck to the Wadi Araba, the great depression which separates the Negev from Jordan. In 1934 he heard Arabs speaking of an area on the east side of the wadi called the Copper Ruin. There he found copper slag and some primitive furnaces. By examining pottery found on the site he was able to date his find to King Solomon's time.

Dr. Glueck found other sites along the Wadi Araba, among them the remains of Solomon's mine at Timna. In 1950 the geologist Dr. Yaakov Bentor discovered copper deposits at Timna which are being mined by Israelis today.

The study of archaeology in Israel may have shed new light on the origins of humanity itself. In the spring of 1960 a farmer working with a bulldozer on a collective settlement just south of Lake Tiberias turned up some strange objects which led to the discovery of fossil remains of the late Lower Pleistocene period, 500,000 to 600,000 years ago. A team from the Hebrew University under Professor Moshe Stekelis undertook careful excavations and brought out of the earth two skull fragments and an incisor tooth of what became known as "Afiqim man," after the name of the settlement. In only three other places—Algeria, Tanganyika and Java—had relics of this kind ever been found. Scholars have concluded from the discovery that Afiqim man did not know how to make fire, and that he was omnivorous. Further study of the site will undoubtedly reveal more about the creature's mode of life and his connection with modern man.

Archaeology has filled in the details of some important historical events. It has been known for some time that in A.D. 132, 62 years after the destruction of the Second Temple, half a million of the Jews of Judea under the leadership of Shimon Bar-Kokhba revolted and were eventually put down after hundreds of thousands of men, women and children had been killed. It was known that the climactic battle took place at Beitar, a fortified hill near Jerusalem. But meanwhile some of Bar-Kokhba's men had withdrawn to the western shore of the Dead Sea. Israeli archaeologists decided to investigate the area around Ein Gedi.

THE people of Bar-Kokhba had barricaded themselves in caves in the faces of some great cliffs. On top of one cliff were ruins of two camps of the Romans, who had besieged the Jews until they perished in the caves below, either by mass suicide or by slow starvation.

Two Bar-Kokhba expeditions were mounted, the first of them in 1960. Yadin led one of the four teams. The entire affair was organized as if it were a military operation, and it turned out to be as packed with high adventure as a polar exploration. The Israeli Defense Forces supplied helicopters to take aerial photographs, and these helicopters hovered in front of first one cliff opening and then another, looking for the caves that might have been inhabited. When likely ones were found, Yadin and other trained archaeologists were let down from the plateau by ropes. They used mine detectors, portable generators, walkie-talkies and field telephones —equipment rarely available to archaeologists.

The Israelis investigated many caves and in one of them found an archaeologist's dream— great amounts of historical material and the remains of some Bar-Kokhba warriors, their skulls piled neatly in baskets. There was no way to tell how the soldiers had died. The investigators found booty that Bar-Kokhba's men had apparently picked up in a raid on some Roman camp. Some of the figures of Roman deities stamped on these objects appeared to have been deliberately scratched and rubbed out, apparently by Bar-Kokhba's men.

MOST important of all, they found a number of documents, mostly on papyrus. They found a Hebrew fragment from the Book of Psalms, written earlier than the year A.D. 100. As they dug deeper and more papyri came to light, Yadin, normally a thoroughly controlled man, became as excited as a small boy. Nearly all the documents were letters from Bar-Kokhba himself, in a fine state of preservation. When the second Bar-Kokhba expedition was staged in 1961, a large number of legal documents was discovered in the same cave. As they were carefully unrolled and read, they began to fill in more and more gaps in history.

Eight miles from Yadin's Cave of Letters, archaeologist Pessah Bar-Adon, in charge of one of the other three groups, dug down through six feet of debris to uncover 432 decorated objects of ivory, stone and copper or bronze. Among them were maces, scepters and crowns, all thought to have been carved by people of the chalcolithic period, who lived around 4000-3000 B.C.

Archaeologists have helped to make settlement in the Negev possible. They found that hundreds of cisterns had been dug in the desert in Judean times to catch and store the runoff of the Negev's infrequent rains. The Judeans had also built stone dams across the wadies, or dry stream beds, to trap soil and rainwater for farming. Mile by square mile the archaeologists explored the Negev. They came to the conclusion that every available acre of tillable land had once been farmed.

The Departments of Geography and Botany of the Hebrew University worked with their archaeologist colleagues studying the system of water controls that had been used in ancient times. Professor Michael Evenari, former vice president of the university and a famed botanist, headed a team that specialized in studying any evidence of ancient agricultural settlements that might apply to the problems of the Negev today. Nelson Glueck earlier had discovered evidence of the agricultural development of a people known as the Nabataeans, who flourished between the Second Century B.C. and the Second Century A.D., and who had inherited and expanded the trade and agriculture of the ancient Israelites. Dr. Glueck found traces of whole villages surrounded by terraced fields and an ingenious system of water control. Dr. Evenari studied hundreds of these farms.

SOON a pattern began to evolve. The fields were in a large central wadi which was fed by tributary wadies, and these were terraced so as to be usable as floodwater catchment areas. Approximately 30 acres of such hill slopes were needed to irrigate each acre of wadi land. Documents were discovered describing the yield of wheat, barley, grapes, dates, figs and vegetables. The secret of the Nabataeans' high yields apparently was in the system they had devised of controlling and directing the flow of water from the slopes onto the wadies.

With the help of foundation funds, Professor Evenari rebuilt two Nabataean farms, restoring all the walls, cisterns and conduits, and planting fruit trees and grain in the bottom land. In 1960 and 1961 other Negev settlements lost their entire winter crop because of drought, but Professor Evenari reported that he had excellent wheat and barley yields, and his fruit orchards were in good condition.

Summarizing his work, Professor Evenari and a colleague reported: "The Nabataeans' conquest of the desert remains a major challenge to our civilization. . . . The age of the machine calls for somewhat different techniques . . . but . . . the best we can do today is no more than a modification of the astute and truly scientific methods worked out more than 2,000 years ago by the Nabataean masters of the desert."

CONFIRMATION by archaeological discoveries of historical passages in the Bible has been important to men and women calling themselves the People of the Book. Archaeology has also written some classic stories that will long be retold. Among the best is the tale of the Dead Sea scrolls.

This exciting series of events began one day in 1947 when two Bedouins, poking around near the north end of the Dead Sea in an area where one of them had earlier lost a goat, entered a dark cave where they found earthen jars containing parchment scrolls. They took the scrolls to nearby Bethlehem and turned them over, presumably for a modest sum, to a local merchant.

Many months later, in the fall of 1947, Professor E. L. Sukenik, then the head of the Hebrew University's Department of Archaeology, received a message from an Armenian antiquities dealer in the Old City of Jerusalem that he had something interesting to show him. Dr. Sukenik was to come at a certain hour to the barbed-wire fence separating two zones of strife-torn Jerusalem. He did so, and the two men talked across the fence. The Armenian had a small piece of parchment, a sample, he said, of some scrolls found by Bedouins in jars in a cave. Would Dr. Sukenik be interested in buying them? The scrolls themselves, he said, were

A RICH INLAY OF LANDMARKS

Archaeological landmarks in Israel's long history are shown at right. Sites dating back to Old Testament times include Hatzor, location of a Canaanite temple; Megiddo, where King Ahab's stables have been found; Apollonia, where Canaanites built a city; Lachish, which contains a walled town conquered by Joshua. Sites dating back to the New Testament era include Capernaum, where Jesus preached; Beit Shearim, which contains the tombs of the Sanhedrin; and Massada, where Herod's palace stands. At Beit Alpha, ancient Jewish mosaics have been found. At Beersheba, 5,000-year-old figurines have been dug up. At Avdat, a Nabataean farm has been restored.

in Bethlehem. If the professor wanted to see them he would have to go there.

Dr. Sukenik returned home and consulted his son, Yigael Yadin. Arab violence had been increasing, and the advice given to his father by Yadin, then Haganah's chief of operations, was a classic of logic and emotion. He said that as a military man he would advise him not to make the trip. As an archaeologist he would urge him to go. As his son he reserved his opinion.

Disguised as an Arab, the father risked his life and went. He was accompanied to Bethlehem by the Armenian intermediary. They met the dealer in an attic, where Dr. Sukenik finally was shown two scrolls. They were still in the jars in which they had been discovered. The professor bought them for the equivalent of $141. That night in his home in the New City of Jerusalem, while the radio was bringing news of the passage of the United Nations partition plan, he examined what he could of the contents of the scrolls. At the time he could not unroll them; this delicate task, which required expert help, was performed later, after he had purchased a third scroll from the same Armenian. The scrolls turned out to contain some Psalm-like hymns, a partial text of the Biblical Book of Isaiah and a hitherto unknown description of an apocalyptic military struggle.

Later Dr. Sukenik learned that four additional scrolls discovered in the same cave by the

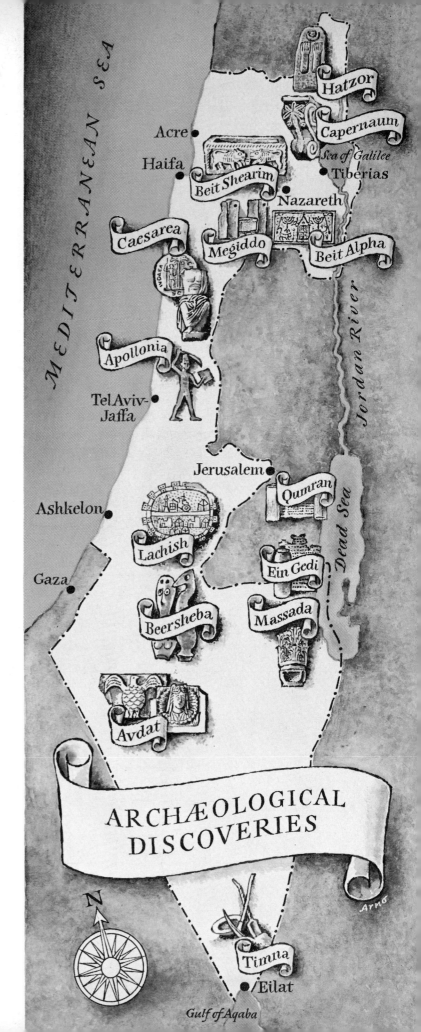

Bedouins had been acquired by the metropolitan of the Syrian Orthodox monastery of Saint Mark in the Old City of Jerusalem. Although Jerusalem was fighting for its life in those days, and the fate of the independence movement was at stake, funds were put at Dr. Sukenik's disposal to buy the other four scrolls. Nevertheless, the metropolitan decided he would do better if he tried to sell them in the United States.

In the spring of 1953, Dr. Sukenik died. A year later Yigael Yadin, by this time out of the army and working again as an archaeologist, was in the United States on a lecture tour when his attention was called to an advertisement in a New York newspaper. The four missing scrolls were being offered for sale by the metropolitan. Cables flew back and forth between Jerusalem and New York, all in code. Every possible effort was made to keep the negotiations secret for fear pressure might be brought to withhold the scrolls from Israeli hands. Finally, through the generosity of D. Samuel Gottesman, a New York industrialist, Yadin succeeded in purchasing all four scrolls for a quarter of a million dollars. At last all seven of them were in the possession of the Israelis.

SCHOLARS everywhere were fascinated by the scrolls. The script varied but was generally neat and readable; it was written in ink on pieces of leather that ranged in length up to almost eight yards. Mistakes were carefully corrected by scribes.

Five of the scrolls reflected the atmosphere and problems of life in the land of Israel at the end of the last century before the Christian era. The other two—called the Isaiah scrolls because one of them contained the entire Book of Isaiah, the other a part of it—are believed to antedate the oldest previously known Hebrew text of the Bible by at least a thousand years. They show that the Bible was more than a sacred legacy two thousand years ago; it was a living force, with direct bearing on problems of the day.

One scroll, which has been named *The Manual of Discipline,* describes a communal group that resembles a Christian monastic order. "Together they shall eat and together they shall pray; together they shall counsel," it states. At the communal meals the religious leader blessed the first portion of the wine or bread.

Dr. Sukenik was the first to point out that the community bore a startling resemblance to that of the Essenes, an ascetic sectarian group who are now generally presumed to be the authors of the scrolls. The historian Pliny had said that the Essenes lived "on the west side of the Dead Sea, above the town of Ein Gedi," the area in which the scrolls were found.

THE most recent addition to the scrolls now in Israel is the Temple Scroll. According to specialist Yadin, the parchment looked like "running chocolate," but despite its deterioration it is the longest and perhaps the most important document found to date. This scroll deals with plans for a temple to be built in the future, and one of its most interesting and surprising aspects is the style in which it is written. The words are in the first person, as if they were spoken by God.

The mass interest of Israelis in the scrolls and other archaeological finds, the attendance of vast numbers of amateurs at conventions of the Israel Exploration Society and the expressed desire of hundreds of people to take part in any archaeological expedition that is announced have amazed professional archaeologists. Wide public interest, for example, was aroused during the early 1960s by the excavation of Ashdod, a site on the Mediterranean coast north of Ashkelon, which contains the remnants of the first Philistine city to be examined by archaeologists; and by diggings at Arad, the first major Biblical site to be excavated in the Negev.

Undoubtedly, there are other discoveries to come. In 1964 a government-established National Archaeological Council began the first country-wide survey of sites. Whatever its findings, it is safe to assume that any new expedition in search of more scrolls or relics will excite as much public attention in Israel as a political crisis or the launching of a rocket.

Near Caesarea, a stone aqueduct erected by Roman legions in the Second Century A.D. stands out imperiously from bone-dry dunes.

A Past Recovered from the Dry Earth

Antiquity is a great morale builder in modern Israel. Among Israelis, invoking past deeds is a favorite way of whipping up enthusiasm for present projects. Soldiers liken themselves to the Maccabees, and Negev colonizers recall the Biblical years in the desert. To make antiquity palpable, Israelis are avidly restoring ancient ruins. Such salvaged landmarks as the ancient town of Caesarea are a welcome proof to Israelis that they are heirs to a uniquely rich past.

HISTORY-DRENCHED RUINS of Caesarea, a port built by Herod the Great in 25-13 B.C., are overlaid with the handiwork of successive waves of conquerors. The broken columns are Roman and the arches were built by early Arab invaders. The curved stonework is part of a Crusader church. The minaret was erected by Turks.

MEDIEVAL MASONRY is part of a tight breakwater built by Crusaders after they wrested Caesarea from the Arabs. Roman columns were used to strengthen the sea wall.

ROMAN MOSAIC in Caesarea (*right*) is cleared of concealing earth with a high-pressure hose. In the elegant imperial port, Pontius Pilate kept his official residence.

EXCAVATORS' FINDS recall the trials and triumphs of a long, turbulent past

WAR CACHE of gold and stone Arab jewelry (*opposite*), buried during an 11th Century crusade, was dug up by Israeli archaeologists from a Roman vault in Caesarea.

NEW TESTAMENT SETTING, a Third Century synagogue at Capernaum has been partly restored by monks. Near this site Jesus performed miracles before Galilee's Jews.

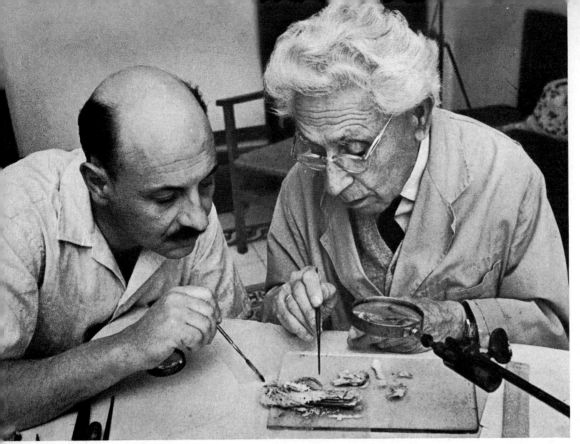

FRAGILE FLAKES of papyrus are examined by Israeli archaeologist Yigael Yadin (*left*) and scroll expert James Biberkraut for the identification of handwriting details.

HISTORIC SCROLLS, part of the first seven found in caves near the Dead Sea in 1947, are on display in Jerusalem. Made of parchment, they are more than 2,000 years old.

COPPER MANUSCRIPTS telling of buried treasure were so brittle they had to be cut into strips to be read. Found at Qumran in 1952, they are now in Jordan's possession.

STURDY MOSQUE of Ahmad al-Jazzar rises above old stone dwellings in the Arab section of Acre. Although Israel's Moslem Arabs have prospered under the Jewish state, their relations with Israeli Jews are often strained.

A
Concern
for Minorities

SAILING down the Mediterranean coast toward Israel from the north, the first major town a traveler sees is ancient Acre, which the Crusaders converted into their main seaport in the 12th Century. The most prominent building in Acre is the Mosque of Ahmad al-Jazzar. Its gleaming dome and needle-thin minaret rear high into the deep blue of the Mediterranean sky. If the wind is offshore and the time is dawn, men at sea can hear the minor-key wail of the muezzin as he calls the followers of Mohammed to morning prayer. A little later, at 6:30 a.m., both passengers and Israelis ashore can listen to passages from the Koran read in Arabic over *Kol Israel*, the state-owned radio.

In Jerusalem the tallest structure is the 152-foot Jesus Tower of the YMCA, in which there are three chapels at various levels for Christians who wish to pause to pray on their way up the 234 steps to the top.

In Haifa, until a luxury hotel was built on the summit of Mount Carmel, the landscape was dominated by the gold dome of a Persian temple built by the Bahais, a world-wide sect which teaches that God's will is periodically manifested through new prophets. Most Bahai adherents are concentrated in the United States and South America, although they look on

Haifa as their religious center. It is the burial place of the forerunner of the religion, Mirza Ali Mohammed, who in 1844 proclaimed himself the herald of a new prophet. In 1863 one Baha-u-llah founded the religion by declaring himself the prophet.

Israel is one of the few nations in the world whose Cabinet includes a minister in charge of religious affairs. The precise translation into English of his title is "Minister of Religions" and not "Minister of Religion," and the distinction between singular and plural is both deliberate and important.

Before 1948 the Jews were a minority everywhere in the world—even in the land of Abraham. Since 1948 the minority has come to be a majority, as a result of the partition of Palestine, the flight of hundreds of thousands of Arabs from the area that is now Israel and the arrival of more than a million Jewish immigrants. Jews now comprise more than 85 per cent of Israel's population.

HOW does a minority people—once it is a majority—treat its own minorities? For the Jews of Israel by far the most important group with which they have to deal consists of Arabs. In a land beset by Arab neighbors who demonstrate little desire to deal on friendly terms, such a minority can present formidable problems.

After the signing of the armistice agreements of 1949 which ended the bitter warfare between Israel and its Arab neighbors, more than 100,-000 Arabs, who for one reason or another had been neither persuaded to flee nor panicked into doing so by their leaders, remained within the boundaries of the new state. In the next 16 years the number nearly tripled, due to the return of 70,000 who had left and to natural increase.

There are many reasons for discontent among the Arab population. Within memory, they had constituted an overwhelming majority in Palestine. It was not easy for them to become accustomed suddenly to a minority status, regardless of how well they might be treated. Under the Ottoman empire and the British Mandate, they

had clearly been Palestine's dominant group.

It was only normal that the Israeli Arabs would resent having to become citizens of a state whose way of life was foreign to their own in almost every conceivable area—religion, culture, economic system, tempo and outlook. But despite the fact that Israeli Arabs were always free to leave, few departed after the initial flight of 1948-1949. The Arabs stayed for a variety of reasons—an attachment to the land which was their home, business interests, family associations, a lack of funds for transportation, a wish to avoid becoming refugees, the unwillingness of most Arab countries to admit them and, in some cases, because they were content with life in Israel.

Neighboring Arab states, especially Egypt, have conducted incessant campaigns seeking to stir up discontent among the Israeli Arabs. In fact, the small Communist party of Israel has managed to gain the bulk of its support from the Arab minority.

Politics and propaganda aside, there are legitimate Arab complaints. Some are psychological, such as the resentment at the use of the word "minority," which is thought by many Arabs to imply inferiority. Other complaints are more specific, such as the often-expressed and probably justified one that it is virtually impossible for an Arab to progress far in the government and sometimes even difficult for Arab high-school graduates to obtain employment.

ALTHOUGH Israeli Arabs are aware, from tuning their radios to Cairo, Damascus and other Arab capitals, that it is Israel's neighbors which do most of the scimitar-shaking and talking about another round of the 1948 war, they nevertheless resented the security measures Israel maintained for many years. Because many of Israel's Arabs live along the borders of the country, they automatically were subject in such areas to what was termed "military government." This meant certain restrictions for all inhabitants of such areas, especially in freedom of movement. Unlike Jews, Israeli Arabs were required to obtain military permission to travel from one city to another after sundown.

The entire question of military government became a political issue in the election campaign of 1961, and arose again in 1962 when Prime Minister Ben-Gurion gave an interview to a reporter in which he was quoted as saying, "The Arabs in Israel enjoy economic, social and educational conditions superior to those in any Arab country, yet they are discontented or hostile toward Israel." More than a few times, Ben-Gurion has publicly suggested that the Arab minority is a potential fifth column inside the country.

In reply to Ben-Gurion's statement, the late Professor Martin Buber, renowned philosopher and professor-emeritus of Hebrew University, joined with other advocates of Jewish-Arab friendship in signing a statement accusing the government of imbuing its Arab inhabitants with a feeling that they are second-rate citizens. The statement called for abolition of "military government in the Arab areas of the country as well as all other forms of discrimination."

The issue eventually came under warm debate in the Knesset. Five separate motions were introduced by different parties, including one from Ben-Gurion's own coalition, calling for the end of military government. Ben-Gurion was strongly opposed. "I regard abolition of the regulations and the military administration," he said, "as abandonment of the state to the intrigues of the enemy in the neighboring countries, and the intrigues of those who hate the state of Israel in this country."

All the motions were defeated (by the narrow margin of four votes each), but Ben-Gurion made concessions: a lifting of the curfew and the granting of freedom-of-movement permits

NON-JEWS IN ISRAEL (PRE-1967)	
Moslems	220,000
Druses	30,000
Greek Catholics	23,000
Greek Orthodox	17,000
Roman Catholics	11,000
Maronites	3,000
Protestants	2,500
Armenian-Gregorians	1,000
Ahmadia	600
Coptics	500
Bahai	200
Abyssinians	50
TOTAL:	308,850

that would remain in effect for a year. Persons who were convicted by a military court were given the right of appealing to a higher military court.

The military courts, for security reasons, have jurisdiction over certain offenses, and there is no right of appeal to the country's civil courts. These offenses include the harboring of fugitives and infiltrators, spying and the carrying of weapons. The principle that there can be no appeal to the civil courts after conviction by one of the military courts for such crimes was upheld by the Israeli High Court in 1951. In times of emergency, the court declared, it was necessary to grant special power "to judge those who jeopardize the security of the state."

At the end of 1966, however, Eshkol abolished the remaining machinery of military government. He announced that there now would be full freedom of movement throughout the country except for restrictions in a few sensitive areas along the borders where everyone would be barred for reasons of security. The functions of the defunct military government were accordingly transferred to the jurisdiction of the civilian authorities.

Modern Israel's first Minister of Religious Affairs was Rabbi Judah L. Maimon, a founder of the Mizrachi religious party, who had been arrested by Russians in the days of the Czar, sentenced to death by Turks in the days of the Ottoman empire and imprisoned by the British in the days of the Mandate. One of his first acts as Minister of Religious Affairs was to go to Nazareth, the village where Jesus grew up and which then, as it happened, contained the largest concentration of Arabs within Israel. Maimon there made a promise: "In every place under our protection, freedom of religion will reign. Our attitude to all religious communities will be one of friendship and respect, and we shall protect all the Holy Places. I trust that . . . friendship will prevail among all sections of the community and that we shall all work together for the good of the country and the welfare of the state. Have we not all one Father? Has not one God created us?''

Some Arabs have, indeed, prospered in Israel. One day recently a handsome young Israeli Arab with his black fur hat set at a jaunty angle stood at the rail on the first-class deck of a ship as it was docking at Haifa. He was returning from an extended pleasure trip around Europe. Pointing down to a large American automobile being lifted from a lower deck, he said, "I could have rented a car in Europe, but it was more fun to have my own." Just at that moment a faultlessly dressed man stepped from a chauffeur-driven car on the dock. "My father!" the young Arab exclaimed, and they waved. The young man pointed to an extensive green area on nearby Mount Carmel. "My father and his brother own most of that land," he said. "We expect to make a great deal of money developing it."

THE Israeli Arabs enjoy full political rights. They have universal suffrage, as do all other Israelis over 18. (In recent elections 85.1 per cent of eligible Arabs voted.) Israeli Arabs may form their own political parties and may run for any political office. A number of Arabs have been elected to the Knesset.

They also enjoy linguistic freedom. Arabic is spoken by 20 to 25 per cent of the total population, and it is recognized as an official language, used with Hebrew on bank notes, coins, road signs and postage stamps. It is the language of the curriculum in all schools for Arab children. Government officials write to Arabs in Arabic. Arab members of the Knesset usually make their speeches in Arabic and are supplied with earphones with which they may listen to a translation of all speeches made in Hebrew.

They have complete freedom to listen. In Acre there are some 7,000 Arabs, mostly skilled workers, fishermen and merchants. Walking through the narrow, dimly lit streets of the outdoor market, with its smell of spices and freshly roasted coffee, one hears from every third or fourth shop the reedy music of the Arab world interspersed with the words of a radio announcer in Cairo, Amman or Damascus denouncing, often in blistering language, the sins and the evils being perpetrated against the "helpless" and "exploited" Arabs of Israel by their Jewish masters. A Jewish policeman saunters by, stops for a moment, listens, then smiles and walks on.

Long before the scheduled start of Israeli television broadcasts in early 1968 sets capable of picking up broadcasts from neighboring Arab countries could be purchased in Israel. The biggest purchasers, when screens became available, were Arab café owners who charged visitors a small fee to watch programs from Beirut and Cairo. In Arab areas of Israel the biggest television attraction is President Nasser of Egypt. When he appears, the Arab cafés are packed and absenteeism from work soars.

Israel's minorities have freedom to read what they please. There is a spot-checking of all mail, but principally to guard against the transmission of secret military information. An Israeli Arab is prevented from writing a letter to his cousin in Cairo or Beirut because Arab countries refuse to accept a letter bearing an Israeli stamp. There is communication between Israelis and citizens of Arab countries, but it must be conducted through intermediaries in neutral areas like Cyprus or Athens.

PAPERS and magazines from all of the important capitals of the world are sold throughout Israel. There is no censorship of such incoming reading material, although there is military censorship of domestic publications. This censorship in theory is confined to preventing the publication of any information of possible military value to Israel's neighbors. During "the Lavon affair," which dominated Israeli politics for many years (see Chapter 5), all references to the security aspects of the matter were killed by the censors, and large blocks of white space appeared in Israeli papers as a result. But political censorship as such is forbidden by law.

If a foreign magazine sold in Israel has a cover story on President Gamal Abdel Nasser of Egypt, copies of the magazine, uncensored, are bought as fast as they are put on the stands. Most of Israel's daily papers subscribe to American, British and French news agency services and in this way get news from the various Arab capitals—which is printed as received. Throughout the 19 years during which Jerusalem was divided, a paper like *The Jerusalem Post* had to rely on an international news agency reporter in the Old City to cover fires or riots occurring only half a mile from its own office, the dispatch traveling thousands of miles to Paris or London and back before it got to the New City of Jerusalem.

THERE was one other way that the two Jerusalems obtained news of each other. Each morning, Israeli and Jordanian frontier guards would hand each other paper parcels. The contents of the package from Jordan—copies of the latest edition of newspapers from all the Arab capitals—were distributed to the editorial offices of Israel's principal papers, and the same thing happened with the copies of Israeli papers that had gone to Jordan.

The Arabs have complete freedom of self-expression. Their many daily, weekly, monthly and quarterly publications are subjected only to military censorship. Several Arab papers and periodicals are Communist organs. They engage in a ceaseless campaign of denouncing the Israeli government, while praising the pronouncements of Nasser and other Arab leaders. These publications are sold on newsstands and distributed through the mail.

Israel grants Arabs the right to travel abroad and some have acted as members of international missions or attended conventions. The Israeli representative to the 1959 conference of the World Federalist Movement in Denmark was Baheej Khleif, an Arab sociologist from Nazareth. Although Jordan for years violated the armistice agreement that was intended to give Israeli Jews the right to visit the Wailing Wall in the Old City, and still with rare exceptions permits no Jews of whatever nationality to cross its borders, Christians crossing from Jordan are admitted into Israel at any time. Israel also permits Christian citizens to enter Jordan to visit places sacred in their religion. Although a few always overstay their time limit, on the excuse of sickness or accident, no one has ever been prevented from returning. The Israeli government has announced on several occasions that it is ready to permit its Moslem citizens to make pilgrimages to Mecca, the birthplace of Mohammed, but neither Saudi Arabia nor the Arab countries through which they would have to pass will agree. There have been a few cases of Israeli Arabs who have obtained the permission of both governments involved to visit ill or dying relatives in a neighboring country.

There is freedom of ownership for the Arabs in Israel, with 80 per cent of the Arab farmers holding title to their own land. In border areas, for security reasons, there has been appropriation of Arab houses and land, but always with compensation offered to the owners.

AS proof that pronouncements about freedom of religion are not meaningless, the government keeps in repair the many mosques that are scattered around the country, sees to it that no large village inhabited by Moslems is without a place of worship and provides some of the mosques with furniture and equipment. Thousands of copies of the Koran have been imported from Turkey to remedy a shortage. The government has also assumed the entire payroll for several hundred imams (spiritual leaders), muezzins (criers to prayer) and caretakers of the country's mosques.

The Arabs have gained economic equality to the extent that they receive wages equal to those paid to other Israelis when working for the government, on public projects or in enterprises conducted by the Histadrut, the national

A Concern for Minorities

labor organization. Under the British Mandate Jews received higher wages than Arabs. In those days Jewish labor leaders made a genuine effort to organize a separate Arab trade union. In 1960 Arabs were accorded full membership in the Histadrut. Within a year, half the Arab working population had registered with the Histadrut. There are now 40,000 Arab members.

THE health of Arabs in Israel has also been improved. The Arabs have the advantage of living in a country that has one doctor for every 440 inhabitants, a ratio unsurpassed anywhere in the world. The rate of infant mortality, so high in other parts of the Middle East because of malnutrition, lack of medical care and poor sanitation, has fallen year by year among Israel's Arabs since the creation of the state, until in 1966 it reached 38.2 per 1,000, the lowest rate in the Arab world.

Arab members of the Histadrut are cared for out of the organization's Sick Fund when they become ill. The Arab tuberculosis rate in Israel is dropping, and those who do suffer from the disease receive free hospitalization and surgery when required. During the years of the British Mandate very few Arab mothers ever went to a hospital to give birth. Now many do, encouraged by the government's policy of paying grants to mothers who give birth in hospitals.

Arabs are covered by a National Insurance scheme from which they receive benefits when they become disabled or when they eventually retire, and the fund pays benefits to their survivors after death.

Arabs in Israel have the right to obtain an education on the same basis as has the rest of the population. During the days of the British Mandate there was one Arab child in school for every 15 Arabs. In Israel today the ratio is one to five (in Saudi Arabia it is reported to be one to 75). There are six times as many Arab schoolteachers today as there were just after independence, although the Arab population has not quite tripled. There are some 380 Arab students enrolled in the Hebrew University and in the Technion, the Israel Institute of Technology.

All of this has been achieved without denigrating Arab culture. Arab libraries have been opened. *Kol Israel* devotes seven and a half hours a day to programs exclusively in Arabic, including a good deal of Middle Eastern music. Films, phonograph records and books in Arabic are regularly imported.

The majority of the Arabs are Moslems, but there are 55,000 Christian Arabs in Israel who make up the bulk of the country's Christian population. The majority of them are members of the Greek Orthodox and Greek Catholic churches, although some belong to the Roman Catholic and Coptic churches. Most Protestant denominations are also represented in Israel among the non-Moslem and non-Jewish population. All the Christians also receive equal treatment.

Christian civil servants are not required to work on Sundays, New Year's Day, Epiphany, Easter Sunday, Easter Monday, Whitsunday, Whitmonday, Ascension Day, Christmas Day and the day following.

The government has built new roads to the several Christian shrines on Mount Tabor, to the Mount of Beatitudes, where Jesus preached the Sermon on the Mount, to Capernaum and to other important Christian religious sites. It has helped with the rebuilding of several churches damaged by shells during the war of 1948, and when St. Michael's Church in Jaffa burned to the ground in 1961, the government offered financial assistance to rebuild it.

THERE are also private gestures of good will from individual Israeli Jews toward Christians. The annual "Hanukkah Toy Fund" of the English-language daily newspaper, *The Jerusalem Post*, sends large crates of toys at Christmas to the children in Christian orphanages and schools. The Jewish National Fund, which plants trees and supervises reforestation throughout the country, makes gifts at the Christmas season of hundreds of Christmas trees to members of the diplomatic corps and to the Christian clergy. The American Protestant evangelist Billy Graham requested—and was granted—permission to speak in all three Israeli cities while on a tour of the Middle East. Although some private groups object, Christian proselytizing is not forbidden.

Mixed marriages between Jews and Christians and, occasionally, between Jews and Arabs have caused some controversy, however. Among immigrants from Poland there were discovered to be about a thousand cases of mixed marriages. If the wife was a Christian, it meant the offspring would not be considered by the rabbis and Orthodox Israelis to be Jews unless converted to Judaism, under the religious definition that assumes a child's religion to be the same as his mother's. The problem of mixed marriages has remained a continuing one, with no easy solution.

BESIDES Moslem Arabs and Christian Arabs, there are several groups of Moslems who are not Arabic in origin: 2,000 Circassians, whose ancestors were first Christians and then were converted to Islam, and 600 members of the Ahmadia, a Moslem sect founded at the end of the 19th Century.

Inhabiting 18 villages in the northern part of Israel are more than 30,000 Druses. They till the soil, speak Arabic and practice a mystical, esoteric religion which they are sworn not to discuss with outsiders, but which is believed to be a mixture of Persian, Christian, Moslem and Hindu elements. Christian Arabs may volunteer, but are not drafted into the Israeli army; the Druses, however, requested some years ago that the males of their group be conscripted. Druse males are now conscripted on the same basis as Jewish Israelis, and many now serve also in the police force. In the wars of 1948 and 1967, they were conspicuous for their bravery. They appear to be the most content of any minority in the country.

The Samaritans are one of the smallest minorities in Israel. There are only some 450 of them in the world—about 300 in Jordan and 150 in Israel. They are the descendants of the settlers transplanted to ancient Israel by the Assyrian kings to take the place of the 10 exiled tribes of the Biblical northern kingdom. There were strong antagonisms between Jews and Samaritans in those days; the parable of the Good Samaritan related in the New Testament reflects these tensions.

In Ramla, a town near Tel Aviv, live the Karaites, Jews who in the Eighth Century refused to accept rabbinical authority. They held that each man could interpret the Bible in his own way and developed their own commentaries on it. They are opposed to intermarriage with other Jews.

There are dozens of Roman Catholic, Greek Catholic, and Greek and Russian Orthodox orders and institutions in the country. Some maintain great stone buildings in Jerusalem. There are 1,200 Catholic and Protestant monks, nuns, priests and ministers, and a hundred more who belong to orders of the Eastern churches. There are Arabs who claim to be descendants of Crusaders, a Catholic priest who once sought and received permission from the Vatican to say part of his Mass in Hebrew and a Baptist congregation that has established a cooperative settlement. The YMCA in mid-December drapes four long strings of colored electric light globes from the top of its high tower. In order to be impartial during the season it lights the bulbs for Christmas and New Year's by the Western calendar, on Christmas and New Year's by the Orthodox Eastern calendar and again on Christmas and New Year's by the Armenian calendar. The YMCA also has an annual party to celebrate the Jewish feast of Hanukkah.

IT is not easy to keep everyone calm and happy in so small a country with so much individualism—with so many different theories as to how man should behave and how God should be addressed. The wonder is that there is as much *shalom* (peace) as there is. It is an indication of the astuteness and wisdom of the majority, as well as of the restraint and good sense of the country's many minorities.

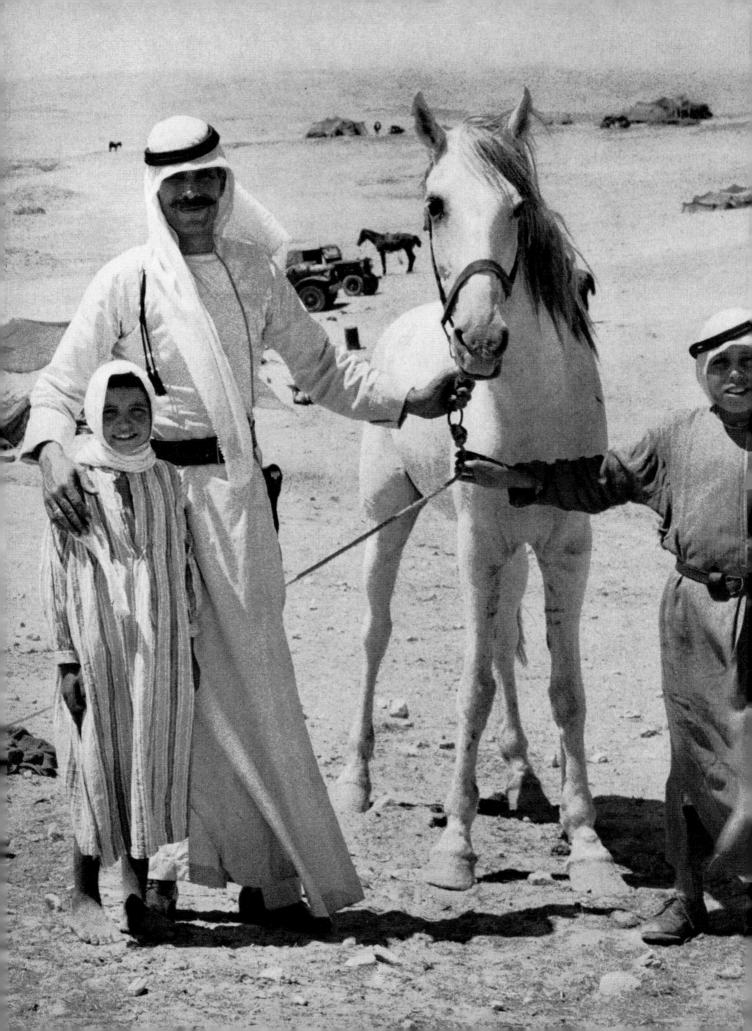

PRINCELY CITIZEN, an Israeli Bedouin sheik stands with his horse and children near the tribal camp *(left)*. Bedouins speak Arabic, and are nomads by tradition.

MUSICAL SHEPHERD, a Bedouin *(right)* follows immemorial custom by playing a pipe as his flock grazes on the Negev, Bedouin herding ground for many centuries.

A Diversity Preserved by Law

In one important way Israel reflects its position in the Middle East. It still preserves some of that colorful mosaic of peoples which is the peculiar trademark of the region, a mosaic consisting of many tiny enclaves of people who follow their own customs undisturbed by the national culture of the majority. In Israel the mosaic survives because the people of such enclaves are left as much as possible to regulate their own internal affairs. Westernized and nationalistic though modern Israel is, it has learned from the Middle East not to concern itself unduly with mere lack of uniformity.

THE DRUSES *are a resolute people who cling to their own unique way of life*

BEWHISKERED SHEIK, Amin Tarif leads Israel's 30,000 Druses, a sect with its own schools and religious courts. Although Arab-speaking, they fought for Israel in 1967.

AUSTERE SHRINE holds a gathering of Druse elders. The Druses, who broke away from Islam in the 11th Century, are forbidden to disclose their religious beliefs.

PIOUS SCRIBE from Yemen carefully repairs an old Torah scroll. The Torah consists of the Five Books of Moses, ultimate source of the laws governing Orthodox life.

ROBED SEXTON in an Orthodox synagogue stands by the Ark of the Law, where the Torah is kept. Services, however, can be held wherever 10 men are gathered.

*LIFELONG STUDY of Judaic law
is thought by the pious to be man's highest
occupation. To those immersed in sacred
books, the secular life of Israel seems remote*

AT HIS PRAYERS, a rabbi wears a ritual shawl and cube-shaped phylactery (*above*) as he studies Leviticus, the third book of the Bible. It is the source of priestly law.

AT HIS SYNAGOGUE, a learned layman devotes himself to unraveling one of the Talmud's subtle legal disquisitions. He may even work out his own interpretation of a law.

BETWEEN SERVICES, members of a congregation use their spare moments to delve into well-thumbed tomes. Many scholars are supported for life by their proud kinsmen.

PARADING TROOPS attract appreciative onlookers in Haifa. Organized in such a way as to discourage the development of a separate military caste, the army is for everyone the proud reason Israel retains its independence.

10

A Maturing Nation

WHEN hundreds of Israeli teenagers one night early in 1962 became so obsessed by the rhythm of a visiting orchestra from Indonesia called The Crazy Strangers that they tore up many of the seats in a theater in Tel Aviv, an older Israeli smiled and remarked, "We're growing up and becoming like other nations."

When the Ministry of Agriculture announced there were now surpluses of some agricultural products, those who remembered the scarcities of earlier days said to one another, "At last we are on our way to becoming a mature, self-sufficient nation."

Watching the country progress, one has the feeling of looking at a movie being run at double speed. Often it is difficult to realize that just a short time ago the Israeli people were still engaged in a struggle for survival.

As Israel each day in more and more ways comes of age, it faces, like an adolescent boy, greater problems but also fresh potentialities.

Increasingly, Israeli leaders become troubled over the division of the population between cities, towns and agricultural settlements. During the days of the British Mandate, when Jews in Palestine were greatly outnumbered by Arabs and when much blood was spilled during riots between Arabs and Jews, life on the land was hazardous. Without the idealism and self-sacrifice of the men and women of the kibbutzim, there might have been little rural development. But the number of kibbutzim and their total population have not been increasing at nearly the rate of the country's growth. Cynics attribute this to a waning of pioneering idealism. Others say it is proof that Israel is maturing: that as a softer and easier way of life becomes available, the majority of people can be expected to take to it.

YET Israel still has a frontier. Ben-Gurion and other leaders repeatedly remind their countrymen that Israel's future is not in the luxury hotels and the coffeehouses of Tel Aviv, but in the south. The challenge they throw out to the young is not universally accepted, nor is it always ignored. At the same time that the *"Espresso* generation" (those who haunt the cafés and coffee shops) were tearing up the seats of a theater under the influence of rock-and-roll music, 120 other young men and women, many just out of the army, were preparing to establish a new cooperative town in the heart of the Negev desert, where life can be rough indeed.

The successful ingathering of more than one million Jews has not decreased the interest of government leaders in further immigration. There are more than 11 million Jews in the world outside Israel: 5.7 million in the United States, 520,000 in France, 450,000 in Great Britain. Only a few thousand from these countries have settled in Israel, because they are content in their own lands. In countries where there is little persecution or discrimination, a motive for leaving is lacking; in countries where there is more discrimination or persecution, the possibility of leaving is lacking. The greatest number of potential immigrants—an estimated 2.5 million—live in Russia, but permission to leave for Israel is denied them. Other groups are the 450,000 in Argentina, 70,000 in Morocco and 120,000 in Romania.

Indeed, after more than a decade of intensive immigration, only 16 per cent of world Jewry

lives in Israel. Government policy is to increase this percentage in every legitimate way, partly because of the need for colonization of the extensive Negev desert, which is difficult to defend as long as it is so sparsely settled, and partly because of the belief of many leaders that the only place that "the Jewishness of Jews" can be preserved is in a Jewish state.

Israel's coming of age has increased rather than diminished the controversy over how far the nation should proceed toward becoming a theocracy—a state directed by religious rather than civil leaders. The tug-of-war between Israeli Jews with differing attitudes toward this question will probably continue as long as there are some who will not use electricity on the Sabbath, others who will listen to the radio on the holy days (but only to religious songs) and still others who declare themselves to have no religion at all. Ben-Gurion has made the flat statement: "We are not and will not be a theocratic state." But on several occasions he had to make concessions to the religious parties to obtain the votes he needed to form a government.

AS Israel grows more mature, progress is being made in creating a rounded economy. But each time doors open somewhere in the Diaspora and a new wave of Jews is permitted to take advantage of the Law of the Return, editorials appear in Israeli papers calling on those already in the country to ease off in their demands for a higher standard of living and prepare to tighten their belts. At the same time those in charge of the country's budget must look for new sources of foreign revenue. For years Israel's financial problems were partly solved by the arrival of a steady flow of heavy equipment and a variety of goods manufactured in Germany, under the $822-million reparations agreement. With this revenue source having disappeared, an all-out effort is being made to stimulate foreign investments in Israeli industry, housing, transport and tourism. The total investment in all of these areas is expected to reach 1.4 billion dollars by the end of 1977. Israeli ingenuity is continuously working on new enterprises to attract foreign money. One day's papers announced three: the raising of minks, the building of "Go Native" motels catering to Americans who have read *Exodus,* Leon Uris' novel about the illegal immigration days, and would like to pretend to relive some of it, and the export of Brahma bulls, of which Israel has a surplus.

ON the negative side, however, the European Common Market has posed grave problems for Israel. In 1966 Israel exported $143 million worth of goods to countries belonging to the Common Market—or more than one third of its total exports. Israel has benefitted from its 1964 most-favored-nation status, but it is currently pressing for associate membership. The source of greatest concern to Israel is the agreement between Common Market countries to drop all customs restrictions between members. This agreement, which is scheduled to be carried out completely by 1972, threatens to put Israel in an almost impossible position in competing with its traditional rivals. But Israel has declared itself ready to revamp its economy in order to realize the maximum possible integration with the Common Market.

In the field of education both the problems and the potentialities are evident. Former Prime Minister Ben-Gurion called on his countrymen to work toward the goal of a free college education for all Israelis. As yet there is not even free secondary schooling, although the government helps pay the cost of a high school education for children of the poor who meet certain high educational qualifications. General disarmament in the Middle East would enable Israel to provide immediate free high school education. Even a substantial cut in the defense budget might make such action possible. But unless there is an easing of tensions between Israel and its neighbors, the extra four years of free schooling may have to wait.

Summing up the country's internal problems, Foreign Minister Abba Eban has remarked,

"Israel is a people to whom nothing is freely given. Its sovereignty, its narrow land, its scanty water, its capital city, the safety of its homes . . . gifts which other nations inherit at their birth, are for us the fruit of . . . contest. [Its] difficulties are the only possessions of Israel which nobody has ever tried to take away. . . . Those who live in siege must either perish or develop attributes to fit their dangers."

Israel's task in its maturity is to maintain the imperturbable spirit that it has manifested in past dangers. When border incidents occur, or when politicians in Arab capitals make inflammatory speeches, there is more nervousness among Israel's friends abroad than in the country itself. No matter what the crisis, life goes on without significant interruption. Pious men read their prayers, ships sail in and out of Haifa Bay and planes depart Lydda Airport for overseas destinations. No matter how frightening the headlines, two million people with a hunger to live like normal human beings in a country of their own go right on doing the dishes, having automobile accidents, engaging in petty backfence squabbles, committing major and minor crimes, making love, getting sick and dying, as everywhere else in the world.

ISRAEL'S coming of age has made it possible for the country to devote more time and money to a goal set by President Chaim Weizmann, himself a scientist, when he said, "We must build a new bridge between science and the spirit of man." In laboratories across the country, men and women in all the branches of science are working to improve the lot of mankind, wipe out disease and prolong the span of human life. These, of course, are among the goals of science everywhere, but in view of Israel's scant resources, the pressure of its pioneering, resettlement and defense problems, such progress as has been made is amazing.

Since Biblical times Jewish prophets and spokesmen have talked of Israel's role "to be a light unto the nations" and to demonstrate brotherhood to the rest of mankind. Less than 10 years after the creation of modern Israel a campaign was started to win friends among the developing nations by extending a helping hand. The passenger list of almost every plane leaving Lydda Airport and every ship sailing out of Haifa includes the names of experts going off to countries that have asked for technical assistance, and when the planes and ships return they bring back trainees who may remain in Israel long enough to become anything from poultry breeders to brain specialists, midwives to machinists. In the decade from 1958 to 1968, Israel welcomed more than 9,000 trainees from 91 countries.

ANOTHER of Israel's potentialities is in the field of medicine. When the new Hadassah-Hebrew University Medical Center was opened on the edge of Jerusalem in 1961, not far from the Israel-Jordan frontier, its director forecast that the day might come when the institution would be a "City of Healing" for Israelis and Arabs of neighboring countries alike. With its high ratio of well-qualified doctors, Israel is uniquely equipped to serve the Middle East in this way.

If cooperation could be achieved between Israel and its neighbors, Israel could begin playing a vital role in the life of the Middle East. Since it has a goodly percentage of specialists trained in the West, the country could help this part of the world realize its industrial potentialities. To irrigate desert land, a country obviously needs both water and pipe. If Israel and Jordan could agree on joint development of the Jordan River, the water problem would be partially solved. Near Haifa, Israel has a pipe factory potentially capable of supplying the needs of its neighbors. Peaceful collaboration could not only help make the desert land in Arab countries as productive as some former desert areas of Israel have become, but a truly viable economic unit might be created. Also, the health and educational standards of the entire Middle East could be raised. But the prerequisite is peace.

It is just that one prize that continues to elude the Israelis. The fact that they have made the desert bloom, that they have built modern cities where only ruins stood before, that they have created a viable democratic society out of chaos and civil war, and that three times in 20 years they have turned back the combined might of their Arab neighbors—all this means little without peace. No matter how often Israel whips its neighbors, so long as the beaten nations continue to refuse them any sort of commerce or recognition there is no victory. Under extraordinary pressure—and surely the Jews have experienced more than their share of that—men may perform superhuman feats, but they cannot keep at it indefinitely.

Following the six-day war in June 1967, Premier Eshkol announced Israel's determination to take a new tack vis-à-vis the Arabs. No longer would Israel rely on the U.N. to act as intermediary and thereby make possible the Arabs' continued pretense that Israel does not even exist: in Israeli eyes, the international body that had in effect set up the Jewish state had, by dint of its repeated failure to protect its charge from Arab intransigence, forfeited all paternal rights. From now on, said Premier Eshkol in an address to the Knesset, Israel would pursue peace only "on the basis of direct negotiations between [Israel] and the Arab states." That alone, he added, "can bring a solution to the problems of the area."

WHETHER that goal can be reached—or how soon it can be reached—may depend not only on the various countries of the Middle East, but also on the attitude of the great powers toward the area and its problems.

But there has never been doubt on the part of any modern Israeli leader about the role that Israel should play. It was David Ben-Gurion who best phrased the timeless goal of the reborn nation: "Our place in the world as a free people will be assured if we help to build a better, juster, kindlier world. Not by wealth, or power, or numbers, but through the examples of our lives shall we help to spread justice and peace among the nations, and thus alone shall we ourselves win peace."

In Jerusalem, Israelis light candles to commemorate the dead. Next page: Children at an Orthodox religious school learn to read.

REVERENTLY AWARE of their unique history, the people of Israel search . . .

. . . for new spiritual goals befitting their ancient traditions, now that they have

won an assured position for themselves among the sovereign nations of the world

Appendix

HISTORICAL DATES

B.C.

c.2000 Abraham, Biblical patriarch to whom Jewish people trace their ancestry, travels from Mesopotamia to the Land of Canaan

c.2000-1700 Abraham's descendants live in Canaan as pastoral nomads

c.1700 Joseph, son of the patriarch Jacob, is sold into slavery in Egypt and eventually rises to become the country's chief administrator. He brings his family to join him, starting off the Israelite settlement in Egypt

c.1700-1290 Israelites remain in Egypt, where they eventually become enslaved

c.1290 Moses leads the Israelites out of Egypt. During their 40 years of wandering they receive the Ten Commandments and establish a basic code of law

c.1250-1225 Conquest of Canaan by Joshua, who leads the various Israelite tribes into the Promised Land after the death of Moses

c.1225-1020 The tribes, loosely federated, are governed by judges and involved in frequent wars

c.1020 Under Saul, the Hebrew tribes establish a monarchy in an effort to resist the expansion of the Philistines

c.1004 Saul is killed in battle with Philistines and the northern and southern groups of tribes are disunited

c.998 David becomes king of the two halves of the kingdom after protracted civil war. Under David, the Philistines are beaten back and Jerusalem becomes the capital. The territory of the kingdom is greatly extended

c.965-926 Reign of King Solomon, David's successor, who erects the Temple of Jerusalem. Trade and commerce bring great prosperity to Israel

c.926 Solomon is succeeded by his son Rehoboam, but the northern tribes secede from the united kingdom. The northern kingdom calls itself Israel and the southern kingdom takes the name Judah

c.734 Israel wars against Judah, which refused to join it in a coalition against Assyria

733-732 Assyria defeats Israel, reducing it to vassalage

721 Defiance of Assyrian rule results in deportation of a large segment of the population of Israel throughout the Middle East. This is the historical basis of the myth of the "ten lost tribes of Israel"

598 Nebuchadnezzar, king of the Babylonians, besieges and conquers Jerusalem

586 To quell a revolt, Nebuchadnezzar once again attacks Judah, thoroughly destroys Jerusalem and its Temple, and deports most of the population to Babylon

c.538 Cyrus, king of the Persians, conquers Babylon and grants Jews permission to return to Jerusalem and rebuild the Temple

520-516 Second Temple is built

334-331 Armies of Alexander the Great march through Middle East. After Alexander's death Judah is absorbed by the Greco-Egyptian kingdom founded by one of his generals

198 Judah comes under control of Seleucid rulers of Syria

c.168 Antiochus Epiphanes of Syria converts the Temple at Jerusalem into a pagan sanctuary

167-164 Revolt against Antiochus led by Judah Maccabee (the Hammerer) liberates Jerusalem; the Temple is cleansed and rededicated

163-160 The Jews are ruled by kinsmen of Judah Maccabee

63 Rome takes over control of Judah

40 Herod, sponsored by Rome, is declared "King of the Jews"

A.D.

c.29 Jesus is crucified at Golgotha

66-70 Revolt of Jews against Roman rule

70 Under Titus, Romans recapture and destroy Jerusalem

132 Final revolt of the Jews against Roman rule is led by Shimon Bar-Kochba

135— The revolt is crushed. Jerusalem is renamed Aelia Capitolina in honor of Rome's emperor, and Jews are prohibited from entering the city.

In successive centuries Palestine, as the area came to be called, is fought over and controlled by many invaders. Its Jewish population dwindles and the Jews disperse into countries all over the world.

In the late 19th Century, after a period of liberalization of anti-Jewish restrictions throughout Europe, political agitation and repressive measures are once again directed against them

1882 Publication of Dr. Leon Pinsker's *Auto-Emancipation*, urging creation of Jewish national home. First Aliyah (wave of immigration) in which several thousand Jews emigrate to Palestine

1896 Theodor Herzl, a journalist, publishes *The Jewish State*, urging establishment of a Jewish state by international agreement

1897 First Zionist congress is held at Basle, organized by Herzl, who becomes father of political Zionism

1903 Anti-Jewish violence in Russia intensifies Jewish interest in settling Palestine

1904-1914 New wave of Jewish immigrants establishes collective agricultural settlements in Palestine

1917 Balfour Declaration. Great Britain declares itself in sympathy with establishment of national home for Jews in Palestine

1923 League of Nations grants Britain mandate over Palestine

1933 Nazis come to power in Germany. Thousands of Jews attempt to emigrate

1936 Arabs riot against Jews in Palestine

1939 Publication of British White Paper on Palestine, restricting Jewish immigration and land purchase

1945 Jewish displaced persons are prohibited from entering Palestine, but they are brought in by undercover operations of Haganah

1947 Great Britain submits the Palestine problem to U.N., which decides to partition the land into Jewish and Arab states. Arabs oppose plan and hostilities break out

1948 Withdrawal of the British. Israeli leaders proclaim the State of Israel. Egypt, Transjordan, Iraq, Syria and Lebanon invade the new nation

1949 Signing of armistice agreements between Israel and the warring Arab states. Chaim Weizmann elected first President of Israel, with David Ben-Gurion as Prime Minister

1949-1951 Immigration brings rapid growth of Israeli population

1955 Egypt organizes commando-style *fedayeen* raiders who terrorize Israeli farm settlements

1956 Israel attacks Egyptian bases in Sinai

1962 Adolf Eichmann executed

1963 Ben-Gurion resigns as Prime Minister and is succeeded by Levi Eshkol

1967 Arab states draw up men and weapons along Israel's borders. Israel pushes Arabs back deep into their own territories.

FOR FURTHER READING

CHAPTER 1: THE LAND AND THE PEOPLE

Baeck, Leo, *This People Israel: The Meaning of Jewish Existence*. Holt, Rinehart and Winston, 1964.

Buber, Martin, *Israel and Palestine*. Farrar, Straus and Young, 1952.

Comay, Joan, *Everyone's Guide to Israel*. Doubleday & Co., 1962.

Elston, D. R., *Israel, the Making of a Nation*. Oxford University Press, 1963.

Frank, M. Z., *Sound the Great Trumpet*. Whittier Books, 1955.

Holisher, Desider, *Growing Up in Israel*. The Viking Press, 1963.

Morris, Yaakov, *Masters of the Desert; 6,000 Years in the Negev*. G. P. Putnam's Sons, 1961.

Parkes, James, *Five Roots of Israel*. Vallentine, Mitchell, London, 1964.

Simon, Leon, ed., *Ahad Ha'Am*. East and West Library, 1946.

Vilnay, Zev, *The Guide to Israel*. Ahiever, Jerusalem, Israel, 1964.

CHAPTER 2: JEWISH HISTORY

Finkelstein, Louis, ed., *The Jews, Their History, Culture and Religion*. Harper & Brothers, 1960.

Glatzer, Nahum, *In Time and Eternity*. Schocken Books, n.d.

Heschel, Abraham J., *The Prophets*. Harper & Brothers, 1962.

The Holy Scriptures. According to the Masoretic Text. Jewish Publication Society, 1960.

Keller, Werner, *The Bible As History in Pictures*. William Morrow & Co., 1964.

Margolis, Max, and Alexander Marx, *History of the Jewish People*. Meridian, 1958.

Roth, Cecil, *The Standard Jewish Encyclopedia*. Doubleday & Co., 1962.

Sachar, Abram Leon, *A History of the Jews*. Alfred A. Knopf, 1965.

CHAPTER 3: ESTABLISHMENT OF ISRAEL

Bein, Alexander, *Theodor Herzl*. Jewish Publication Society, 1941.

Crossman, Richard H. S., *A Nation Reborn*. Atheneum, 1960.

Elbogen, Ismar, *A Century of Jewish Life*. Jewish Publication Society, 1964.

Halpern, Ben, *The Idea of the Jewish State*. Harvard University Press, 1961.

Herzl, Theodor, *The Jewish State*. M. Newman, Tel Aviv, 1956.

Hess, Moses, *Rome and Jerusalem*. Philosophical Library, 1958.

Joseph, Dov, *The Faithful City; The Siege of Jerusalem, 1948*. Simon and Schuster, 1960.

Kimche, Jon and David, *A Clash of Destinies*. Frederick A. Praeger, 1960.

Koestler, Arthur, *Promise and Fulfilment, Palestine 1917-1949*. Macmillan, 1949.

Lorch, Netanel, *The Edge of the Sword; Israel's War of Independence, 1947-1949*. G. P. Putnam's Sons, 1961.

Marshall, General S.L.A., *Sinai Victory*. William Morrow, 1957.

Robinson, Jacob, *Eichmann and the Jewish Catastrophe*. Macmillan, 1965.

Sachar, Howard M., *The Course of Modern Jewish History*. World, 1958.

St. John, Robert, *Ben-Gurion*. Doubleday & Co., 1959.

Weizmann, Chaim, *Trial and Error: The Autobiography of Chaim Weizmann*. Harper & Brothers, 1949.

CHAPTER 4: INGATHERING OF THE EXILES

Agar, Herbert, *The Saving Remnant*. Viking Press, 1960.

Baer, Yitzhak, *Galut*. Schocken Books, 1947.

Goitein, S. D., *From the Land of Sheba; Tales of the Jews of Yemen*. Schocken Books, 1947.

Hazaz, Hayim, *Mori Sa'id*. Abelard-Schuman, 1956.

Heschel, Abraham J., *The Earth Is the Lord's*. Abelard-Schuman, 1956.

Sachar, Howard Morley, *Aliyah; The Peoples of Israel*. World, 1961.

CHAPTER 5: GOVERNMENT AND POLITICS

Eytan, Walter, *The First Ten Years*. Simon and Schuster, 1958.

Kraines, Oscar, *Government and Politics in Israel*. Houghton Mifflin, 1961.

McDonald, James G., *My Mission in Israel. 1948-1951*. Simon and Schuster, 1951.

Pearlman, Moshe, *The Capture and Trial of Adolf Eichmann*. Weidenfeld and Nicolson, London, 1961.

Safran, Nadav, *The United States and Israel*. Harvard University Press, 1963.

Syrkin, Marie, *Golda Meir: Woman with a Cause*. G. P. Putnam's Sons, 1963.

CHAPTER 6: THE ECONOMY

Baratz, Joseph, *A Village by the Jordan: The Story of Degania*. Sharon Books, 1957.

Darin-Drabkin, H., *The Other Society*. Harcourt, Brace & World, 1962.

Halperin, Haim, *Agrindus: Integration of Agriculture and Industries*. Routledge & Kegan Paul, 1963.

Rubner, Alex, *Economy of Israel*. Frederick A. Praeger, 1960.

Spiro, M. E., *Kibbutz, Venture in Utopia*. Schocken Books, 1964.

CHAPTER 7: RELIGION AND THE ARTS

Agnon, S. Y., ed., *Days of Awe*. Schocken Books, 1948.

Baeck, Leo, *Judaism and Christianity*. Jewish Publication Society, 1958.

Bergman, Samuel H., *Faith and Reason; An Introduction to Modern Jewish Thought*. Hillel, 1961.

Epstein, Isidore, *The Faith of Judaism*. Soncino Press, London, 1954.

Gradenwitz, Peter, *The Music of Israel*. W. W. Norton, 1949.

Halkin, Simon, *Modern Hebrew Literature*. Schocken Books, 1950.

Hochhuth, Rolf, *The Deputy*. Grove Press, Inc., 1964.

Roth, Cecil, ed., *Jewish Art*. McGraw-Hill, 1961.

St. John, Robert, *Tongue of the Prophets*. Dolphin Books, Doubleday, 1952.

Scholem, Gershom G., *Major Trends in Jewish Mysticism*. Schocken Books, 1941.

Weiner, Herbert, *The Wild Goats of Ein Gedi*. Doubleday, 1961.

CHAPTER 8: ARCHAEOLOGY OF THE HOLY LAND

Albright, William Foxwell, *The Archaeology of Palestine*. Penguin Books, 1960.

Avi-Yonah, Michael, and E. G. Kraeling, *Our Living Bible*. McGraw-Hill, 1962.

Glueck, Nelson, *Deities and Dolphins*. Farrar, Straus & Giroux, 1965. *Rivers in the Desert*. Jewish Publication Society, 1959.

Pearlman, Moshe, and Yaacov Yannai, *Historical Sites in Israel*, Massada-P.E.C. Press, Ltd., Israel, 1964.

Schubert, Karl, *The Dead Sea Community*. Harper & Brothers, 1959.

Wright, G. Ernest, *Biblical Archaeology*. The Westminster Press, 1961.

CHAPTER 9: A MINORITY'S MINORITIES

The Arabs in Israel. Israel Ministry for Foreign Affairs, Information Department, Jerusalem, 1961.

Pickthall, Mohammed Marmaduke, trans., *The Meaning of the Glorious Koran*. Mentor, 1953.

Pinner, Walter, *How Many Arab Refugees?* MacGibbon, London, 1959.

CHAPTER 10: A MATURING NATION

Ben-Gurion, David, *Israel: Years of Challenge*. Holt, Rinehart and Winston, 1963.

Buber, Martin, *Israel and the World*. Schocken Books, 1948.

Eban, Abba, *Voice of Israel*. Horizon Press, 1957.

Elath, Eliahu, *Israel and Her Neighbors*. World, 1957.

Hurewitz, J. C., *Diplomacy in the Near and Middle East*. Princeton University Press, 1956.

Janowsky, Oscar I., *Foundations of Israel: Emergence of a Welfare State*. D. Van Nostrand, 1959.

Kreinin, Mordechai E., *Israel and Africa, A Study in Technical Cooperation*. Frederick A. Praeger, 1964.

Prittie, Terence, *Israel*. Frederick A. Praeger, 1967.

MAJOR HOLIDAYS IN ISRAEL

NAME AND DATE CELEBRATED	PURPOSE
ROSH HASHANAH (THE NEW YEAR). Celebrated on the 1st and 2nd of Tishri, a month which falls during September and October.	A time of spiritual renewal. Tradition holds that Rosh Hashanah is the beginning of a period when God judges men and decides what their destinies will be during the coming year. A principal feature of the holiday is the blowing of the *shofar*, or ram's horn, which summons men to self-judgment.
YOM KIPPUR (THE DAY OF ATONEMENT). Tishri 10th.	The holiest day of the year, on which Jews spiritually rededicate themselves. Yom Kippur is marked by prayer and fasting.
SUCCOT (THE FEAST OF TABERNACLES). Tishri 15th.	Commemorates both the 40-year wandering of the Israelites in the wilderness and the summer harvest. The holiday has five symbols: the palm, the citron, the myrtle and the willow, which are carried in synagogue processions, and the *succah*, an outdoor structure in which families traditionally sleep and take meals. Its roof, made of tree branches, recalls the temporary dwellings erected at harvest time and those in which the Jews lived during the wandering.
SHEMINI ATZERET—SIMCHAT TORAH (8TH DAY OF ASSEMBLY—THE REJOICING OF THE LAW). Tishri 22nd.	Concluding autumn festival, it marks the completion of the annual cycle of readings from the Torah. Members of the congregation joyously carry the sacred Torah scrolls in procession through the synagogue.
HANNUKAH (THE FEAST OF LIGHTS). Celebrated for eight days extending from Kislev (November-December) 25th to Tevet (December-January) 2nd.	Recalls the victory of Judah Maccabee over Syrian forces and the subsequent purification and rededication of the Temple in 164 B.C. Candles are lighted every day during the holiday to commemorate the relighting of the Temple lamps.
TU B'SHEVAT (THE NEW YEAR FOR TREES). Shevat (January-February) 15th.	Celebrates the rising of the sap in the fruit trees. On Tu B'Shevat it is customary to plant saplings and to eat almonds, figs and carob, the fruit of the locust tree.
PURIM (THE FEAST OF LOTS). Adar (February-March) 15th.	One of the merriest days in the year, it commemorates the courage of Queen Esther, who interceded with her Persian husband, King Ahasuerus, to prevent a planned slaughter of his Jewish subjects. Parades and fancy-dress parties are held on Purim.
PESACH (PASSOVER). Nisan (March-April) 15th to 21st.	A commemoration of the exodus from Egypt. *Matzot*, or unleavened bread, symbolizing the unprepared dough which the Israelites took with them as they left, is eaten during the week of Pesach and at the *seder*, a ritual dinner at which the story is recounted.
YOM HA'ATZMAUT (ISRAELI INDEPENDENCE DAY). Iyar (April-May) 5th.	Anniversary of the proclamation of the state in 1948.
LAG B'OMER (33RD DAY OF THE OMER). Iyar 18th.	Celebrated on the 33rd of the 49 days separating Pesach from Shavuot, Lag B'Omer honors both the anniversary of the death, in the Second Century, of Rabbi Simeon Ben-Yohai, reputed author of a famous mystical work, the *Zohar,* and the association of the Rabbi Akiva and his disciples with the rebellion of Bar-Kokhba against the Romans. There are bonfires, archery displays and an all-night pilgrimage to Rabbi Simeon Ben-Yohai's tomb at Meiron.
SHAVUOT (THE FEAST OF WEEKS). Sivan (May or June) 6th.	Celebrated at the traditional time of the wheat harvest, Shavuot commemorates the presentation of the Ten Commandments to Moses. The Book of Ruth, which mentions the ancient barley and wheat harvests, is read in the synagogues.
TISHA B'AV (THE 9TH OF AV). Av (July-August) 9th.	A fast day, Tisha B'Av commemorates the destruction of the First and Second Temples. In the synagogue the Book of Lamentations is read, dirges are sung and mourning customs are observed.

FAMOUS ISRAELI CULTURAL FIGURES AND THEIR PRINCIPAL WORKS

ART AND SCULPTURE

Schatz, Boris	1866-1932	Leader of Israel's artistic renaissance. Founded Bezalel Art School and Museum, Jerusalem
Steinhardt, Jacob	1887-	Powerful woodcuts on European Jewish themes and the Old Testament
Zaritzky, Joseph	1891-	Fresh and spontaneous abstract canvases
Rubin, Reuven	1893-	Colorful paintings of the landscapes and peoples of Israel
Janco, Marcel	1895-	Founder of Israel's artists' village, Ein-Hod. Still lifes and stylized Near Eastern landscapes
Ticho, Anna	c.1895-	Serene drawings of Jerusalem and Israeli landscapes executed in meticulous classical style
Ardon (Bronstein), Mordekhai	1896-	Images drawn from Jewish legend and mysticism: *Steppes of the Negeb, The Story of a Candle*
Levanon, Mordecai	1901-	Figure paintings and mystical expressionist landscapes
Mokady, Moshe	1902-	Dark-toned expressionist canvases of early years now grown lighter and abstract
Ben-Zvi, Zeev	1904-1952	Sculpture: portraits with cubistic elements of famous Israelis; metal sculpture

ARCHITECTURE

Rau, Heinz	1896-1965	Synagogue, Hebrew University, Jerusalem; private dwellings
Rechter, Zeev	1899-1960	Mann Auditorium, Tel Aviv; Faculty of Archaeology building, Hebrew University
Sharon, Arie	1900-	Winston Churchill Auditorium, Haifa; Israel pavilion, Brussels World Fair
Carmi, Dov	1905-1962	The Histadrut building, Tel Aviv; one of main architects for new Knesset buildings, Jerusalem
Mansfeld, Alfred	1912-	National Museum of Art and Archaeology, Jerusalem; one of main architects for Technion (Israel Institute of Technology) buildings, Haifa
Elhanani, Arie	1918-	Israel pavilion, Brussels World Fair; one of main architects for Weizmann Institute of Science buildings, Rehovoth
Klarwein, Joseph	1893-	One of main architects for new Knesset buildings; stadium, Hebrew University

MUSIC

Edel, Yitzhak	1896-	Cantatas, songs, chamber music, orchestral works
Ben-Haim, Paul	1897-	Symphonies, chamber music, piano music, choral works
Kaminski, Joseph	1903-	*Concertino* for solo trumpet and orchestra. Chamber music
Lavry, Marc	1903-1967	Oratorio: *The Song of Songs.* Symphonies, symphonic poems, operas, songs and dance pieces
Boscovich, Alexander Uriyah	1907-1964	Cantata: *Daughter of Israel.* Suites for orchestra and for piano. Concerto for oboe and orchestra
Partos, Oedoen	1907-	Symphonic fantasy: *Ein Gev.* Chamber music, orchestral music, concertos
Avidom, Menahem	1908-	Symphonies: *Folk Symphony, David Symphony, Symphony Number 7.* Chamber music, songs
Jacoby, Hanoch	1909-	*King David's Lyre* for small orchestra. Chamber music, songs, symphonies
Tal (Gruenthal), Joseph	1910-	Cantatas, piano music, violin music, songs
Lakner, Yehoshua	1924-	Piano music, songs, flute music
Orgad (Buschel), Ben-Zion	1926-	Orchestral works, choral music. Song cycle: *Tagore Songs*

LITERATURE

Ahad Ha-Am (Ginzberg)	1856-1927	Essays: *Al Parashat Derakhim* (At the Crossroads)
Bialik, Hayyim Nahman	1873-1934	Poetry: *Kol Shirei . . .* (Poetry of . . .). Short stories: *Aftergrowth and Other Stories.* Essays
Klausner, Joseph	1874-1958	History: *Historia shel Ha-Sifrut Ha-Ivrit Ha-Hadasha* (History of Modern Hebrew Literature), *Jesus of Nazareth, From Jesus to Paul*
Tchernichovsky, Saul	1875-1943	Poetry: *Shirim* (Poems), *Idiliot* (Idyls). Translations: *The Iliad, The Odyssey, Oedipus the King*
Buber, Martin	1878-1965	Philosophy and theology: *I and Thou, The Prophetic Faith, Israel and the World, Hasidism*
Fichman, Yaakov	1881-1958	Poetry: *Demuyot Kedumim* (Images Out of Antiquity). Criticism
Kabak, Abraham A.	1881-1944	Novels: *Ba-Mish'ol Ha-Tzar* (On the Narrow Path), *Shlomo Molkho*
Kahan, Yaakov	1881-1960	Poetry: *Shirim* (Poems). Drama: *Ketavim Dramatiim* (Dramatic Works)
Burla, Yehuda	1886-	Novels: *Alilot Akavia* (The Adventures of Akavia), *Kissufim* (Yearning). Short stories
Ha-Meiri, Avigdor	1886-	Novels: *Ha-Shigaon Ha-Gadol* (*The Great Madness*). Short stories. Poetry
Shimeoni, David	1886-1957	Poetry: *Shirim, Poemot, Idiliot*
Shneur, Zalman	1887-1959	Poetry: *Gesharim* (Bridges). Novels: *Pandre Ha-Gibbor* (Pandre the Mighty). Short stories
Agnon, Shmuel Yosef	1888-	Novels: *The Bridal Canopy, Ore'ah Nata Lalun* (An Overnight Guest). Short stories
Kaufmann, Yehezkel	1889-1964	Social history: *Gola ve-Nekhar* (Exile and Estrangement), *The Religion of Israel*
Greenberg, Uri Zvi	1894-	Poetry: *Rehovot Ha-Nahar* (Wide River)
Hazaz, Hayyim	1897-	Novels: *Ya'ish, Ha-Yoshevet Ba-Ganim* (*Mori Sa'id*). Short stories. Drama
Halkin, Simon	1899-	Poetry: *Al Ha-I* (On the Island). Translation: *Leaves of Grass.* Novels. Criticism
Lamdan, Yitzhak	1900-1954	Poetry: *Masada, Be-Maale Akrabim* (Up Scorpions' Ascent)
Shlonsky, Avraham	1900-	Poetry: *Avnei Bohu* (Desolate Rocks), *Al Milet* (Well Set)
Pinkerfeld-Amir, Anda	1902-	Poetry: *Gadish va-Omer* (A Heap and a Sheaf)
Shalom, Sh.	1905-	Poetry: *Sefer Ha-Shirim ve-Ha-Sonetot* (Poems and Sonnets)
Goldberg, Leah	1911-	Poetry: *Mukdam u-Me'uhar* (Early and Late). Drama: *Baalat Ha-Armon* (Lady of the Manor)
Bar-Yosef, Yehoshua	1912-	Novels: *Ir Kesuma* (Enchanted City), *Em Ha-Banot* (The Mother of the Daughters). Short stories
Yizhar, S.	1920-	Novel: *Yemei Tziklag* (The Days of Tziklag); Short stories: *Arbaa Sippurim* (Four Stories)
Shamir, Moshe	1921-	Novels: *Melekh Basar va-Dam* (*A King of Flesh and Blood*). Short stories. Dramas

Credits

The sources for the illustrations in this book are shown below. Credits for pictures from left to right are separated by commas, top to bottom by dashes.

Cover: David Rubinger
8—Paul Schutzer for LIFE INTERNATIONAL
10 through 13—Drawings by Shelly Fink
15—Joe Nettis
16—Paul Schutzer for LIFE INTERNATIONAL
17—A. Louis Goldman from Rapho Guillumette
18—Jerry Cooke for SPORTS ILLUSTRATED
19—Burt Glinn from Magnum
20 through 23—A. Louis Goldman from Rapho Guillumette
24—Eric Schaal © Hadassah Medical Relief Association, 1961
29—Map by Enrico Arno
31 through 35—Dr. Roman Vishniac
36—Zionist Archives and Library
43—Map by Rafael Palacios
46, 47—Culver Pictures except top right Collection of Tim Gidal
48, 49—United Press International, Frank J. Scherschel
50, 51—Government of Israel, Gamma-Pix—Cornell Capa from Magnum, Caron for Gamma-Pix
52—Cornell Capa from Magnum—T. Spencer
53—Caron for Gamma-Pix—Leonard Freed
54—David Rubinger
59—Chart by Bill Dove
61 through 63—United Jewish Appeal
64—Joe Nettis—Erich Hartmann from Magnum
65—Burt Glinn from Magnum
66, 67—Jerry Cooke
68—Burt Glinn from Magnum
75—David Harris
76, 77—Left David Rubinger, right David Harris—United Press International
78, 79—David Rubinger

80, 81—David Rubinger except right Gjon Mili
82—Erich Hartmann from Magnum
90—Werner Braun
91—Werner Braun—Rolf Kneller
92—Z. Kluger from Black Star
93—Jerry Cooke
94—David Rubinger
95—David Seymour from Magnum—Leni Sonnenfeld
96—Leni Sonnenfeld
97—Burt Glinn from Magnum
98, 99—A. Louis Goldman from Rapho Guillumette
100—Courtesy Yale University
108—Paul Schutzer for LIFE INTERNATIONAL
109—Werner Braun
110, 111—Leni Sonnenfeld
112—Alfred Eisenstaedt
113—Burt Glinn from Magnum, David Rubinger
114, 115—David Rubinger
119—Map by Enrico Arno
121, 122, 123—Pierre Boulat
124—David Rubinger
125—A. Louis Goldman from Rapho Guillumette
126, 127—Top left David Rubinger
128—A. Louis Goldman from Rapho Guillumette
136, 137—Leni Sonnenfeld, William H. Greene from Photo Researchers, Inc.
138, 139—A. Louis Goldman from Rapho Guillumette
140—Paul Schutzer for LIFE INTERNATIONAL
141—James Whitmore
142, 143—Alfred Eisenstaedt except left James Whitmore
144—A. Louis Goldman from Rapho Guillumette
149—James Whitmore
150, 151—Paul Schutzer for LIFE INTERNATIONAL

ACKNOWLEDGMENTS

The editors of this book are indebted to the following persons, all of whom read and commented on portions of the text: Dr. Ben Halpern, Associate Professor of Near Eastern Studies, Brandeis University; Rabbi Herbert Weiner of Temple Israel, South Orange, New Jersey; Rabbi Eugene J. Duschinsky, formerly of the Jewish Agency for Israel; Israeli Consuls Haim Zohar, Moshe Aumann, Yehuda Avner and Malka Ben-Yosef; and Rinna Samuel of the Weizmann Institute, Rehovoth, Israel.

Index

This symbol in front of a page number indicates a photograph or painting of the subject mentioned.

Elijah, 12
England, medieval, 30
Ephraim, 27
Esau, 26
Eshkol, Levi, 70, 72, *75, 88, 131, 148
Essenes, 120
Europe, exports to, 88, 147
European Jews: ghetto life of, *31-35; migration to Israel since 1948, *54, 55-56, 58; migration to Palestine before 1948, 38, 39, 55; 19th Century, 38, 55; persecution of, 30, 38, 40, 41; refugees, 40, 41, 56; religious traditions of, 102
Evenari, Michael, 118
Exile, 10, 30, 37-38; Babylonian, 28, 103; ghetto life, *31-35
Exodus, 27, 57
Exodus, Uris, 147
Exports, 10, 89, 147; farm products, 86, 88; industrial, 89; minerals, 14, 83, 96
Ezekiel, 10, 28, 86

Faluja, 44
Farming. *See* Agriculture
Fertile Crescent, 25
Food production, 86
Foreign investment, 89, 146-147
Foreign trade. *See* Exports
Forest of the Martyrs, 84
Forestry, 84, 134
France, 30, 69, 146

Gadna, 74
Gal, Uzi, 89
Galilee, 39, 111, 125; irrigation in, *94-95; Sea of, 14, *18, 85, 86, *91, 94; village in, *19
Gaza, 27, 44, 52
Gaza Strip, raids from, 45, 52
Gdudei Noar, 74
Germany, 39, 40, 56, 84, 102; persecution of Jews in, 40, 41, 73-74; reparations from, 44-45, 146
Ghettos, 30, *31-35, 56
Gilead, 27
Glueck, Nelson, 60, 116, 118
Goliath, 14, 27
Gomorrah, 87
Gottesman, D. Samuel, 120
Government, 44, 70-72, 146; instability of, 70; military, of border areas, 130-131
Graham, Billy, 135
Great Britain, 26, 69, 74, 88; immigration restriction by, 40, 56; number of Jews in, 146; Palestine Mandate of, 39-41, 73, 107, 130, 134; Palestine policy of, after World War II, 40-42, 49; promises independent Arab state, 39, 40; in Suez crisis, 45;

supports Zionism, 39, 47; withdrawal of, from Palestine, 12, 42, 49
Greek Orthodox church, 131, 134, 135
Greeks, 12, 28; Catholics, 131, 135
Gregorian Armenians, 131

Hacham, Amos, 103
Hadassah, 25
Hadassah-Hebrew University Medical Center, 42, 107, 148; synagogue, *24, 101, 107
Haganah, 40-41, 42, 74, 119
Haifa, 12, *66-67, 103, 105, 106, 129-130, *144; Jewish-Arab strife in, 41; mentioned, 10, 148; oil refineries at, 84
Hanukkah, 30, 134, 135
Haran, 26
Hassidism, 102; followers of, *16
"Hatikvah," 42
Hatzor, 119
Hazaz, Haim, 106
Health, 107, 134
Hebrew: alphabet, *table* 105; language, 11, 39, 45, 56, 71, 102, 103-104, 111, 132; origin of word, 26
Hebrew Union College, 116
Hebrew University, 13, 47, 103, 105, 111, 134; archaeological work, 117, 118; Medical Center, 42, 107, 148; synagogue, *24, 101, 107
Hermon, Mount, 12
Herod, King, 14, 30, 115, 119, 122
Herut party, 44, 71
Herzl, Mount, 84
Herzl, Theodor, 38, *46, 84
Herzliya, *21
Herzog, Haim, *78-79
High Court of Justice, 73, 131
Histadrut, 72, 88-89, 133-134
History, 9, 25-30, 115-120; Caesarea, 115, 121-124; exile, 30, 31, 37-38; Roman period, 30; Second Century Jewish Revolt, 30, 114, 117
Hitler, Adolf, 40
Holidays, religious, 30, 102-103, 134, 135
"Homeland," choice of, 26, 30, 38
Housing: of immigrants, 14, 57-58, 62; urban, *20, *62, *98-99
Hula Basin, 86
Hungary, 56
Husseini, Haj Amin el, 39

Ibri(m), 26
Imams, 133
Immigrants, *54, 55-57, *61-67, 83, 135; assimilation of, 58, 61, 69-70, 71, 74, 104, 111; economic absorption of, 56, 84; kibbutzim founded by, 85;

"Orientals," 58; potential, 146
Immigration, 130; agricultural movement, *36, 38, 75, 85; British restriction of, 40, 42, 56; First Aliyah, 38; preparations for future, 14, *62-63, 146; problems of, 57-58, *61-63; restrictions lifted, 42, 55; Second Aliyah, 39; since 1948, 15, 44, 55-57; after World War I, 39-40
Income, *table* 88, 133-134
Independence, proclamation of, 42, *49, 55, 60
Industry, 12, 88-89, *96-97
Infant mortality rate, 107, 134
Insurance, for Arabs, 134
Investment, capital, 89, 146-147
Iran, 56
Iraq, 43, 44, 56, 58, 71, 84
Irgun, 40, 41-42, 44, 71, 74
Irrigation, 14, 86, *94-95, 148; ancient system of, 118
Isaac, 26, 27, 28
Isaiah, 56; scrolls, 119, 120
Islam, 73, 138
Israel (Jacob), 26
Israel: area of, 9-10, 14, *map* 43; choice of name, 42; Kingdom of, 28, *map* 43; non-Jews in, *table* 131; 12 tribes of, 25, 26, 27, 28
Israel Exploration Society, 120
Israel Freedom Fighters, 40
Israel Institute of Technology, 105, 111, 134
Israel Society for Bible Research, 103
Italy, 56

Jacob, 26, 27
Jaffa, 12, 38, 40, 42, 58, 134
Jebusites, 27
Jeremiah, 28
Jericho, 14, 27
Jerusalem, *17, *22-23, *map* 29, 101, 103, 105, 116, 129, 148, 149; description of, 13, 106-107; divided city, 13, 22, 44, 118, 133; during 1948 war, 12-13, 43, 55, 105; first destruction of, 28, 56; historical mentions of, 27, 39; history of, 12-13, *map* 29; internationalization plan for, 12, 41, 44; Israeli capital, 13, 44; Jewish hope for restoration of, 10, 37-38; mentioned, 10, 45, 64, 74, 76, 80, 84, 85, 86, 118, 120, 135; Roman destruction of, 11, 30; terrorist acts in, 41, 42, *48-49
Jerusalem Post, The, 133, 134
Jesus, 12, 14, 30, 56, 119, 125, 131, 134
Jewelry, ancient, *124
Jewish Agency, 39, 40, 41, 42, 57, 59, 104
Jewish National Fund, 38, 84, 134
Jewish State, The, Herzl, 38

Jew(s): anti-Arab retaliatory acts of, 41-42; anti-British acts of, 40-41; defined, 102; history of, 25-30; origin of word, 28. *See also* World Jewry
Jezreel Valley, 14
John the Baptist, 107
Jonah, 12
Jordan, 10, 44, 45, 60, 71, 126, 133, 135, 148; annexes Old City of Jerusalem, 13, 44, 105; communications with, 133; mentioned, 27, 116. *See also* Transjordan
Jordan River, 26, 27, 86, 148; Valley, 83
Jordan Water Project, 86, *94
Joseph, 26
Joshua, 14, 27, 119
Judah, 27, 86; Kingdom of, 28, 30
Judah Maccabee, 28
Judaic Law, 27, 28, 30, 73, 101, 102, 140, 142
Judaism, 102-103. *See also* Orthodox Judaism
Judea, 14, 117, 118; Roman satellite, 30
Judean hills, 13, 14, 84
Judges, period of, 27
Juvenile delinquency, 60

Karaites, 135
Khamsin, 83, 106
Khleif, Baheej, 133
Kibbutzim, *36, 58, 85, 86, 146; life in, *90-91, *93
King David Hotel, 41
Kinneret, Lake. *See* Galilee, Sea of
Knesset, 17, 44, 55, 60, 70, 71, *76-77, 85, 88, 102, 104, 106, 131, 132; Gedola, 70
Kol Israel, 103, 129, 134
Koran, 129, 133
Kurds, 58

Labor federation. *See* Histadrut
Labor party. *See* Mapai
Lachish, 119
Land: ownership, Arab, 133; reclamation, 85, 86-87, *94
Landscape, 84, 85, 106
Languages, 11, 104, 132. *See also* Arabic; Hebrew
Lavon, Pinhas, 72, 132
Law: ancient Jewish, 27, 30, 73, 102, 140, 142; electoral, 71; immigration, 55; present system of, 73-74
League of Nations, 39, 40
Lebanon, 10, 12, 43, 44
Liberal party, 71
Liberation, War of, 14, 43-44, 84, 105, 116; technically still on, 10, 45
Life expectancy, 107
Literature, 11, 106, 108
Lot, 86

XXXX

Production staff for Time Incorporated

John L. Hallenbeck (Vice President and Director of Production)

Robert E. Foy, Caroline Ferri and Don Sheldon

Text photocomposed under the direction of

Albert J. Dunn and Arthur J. Dunn

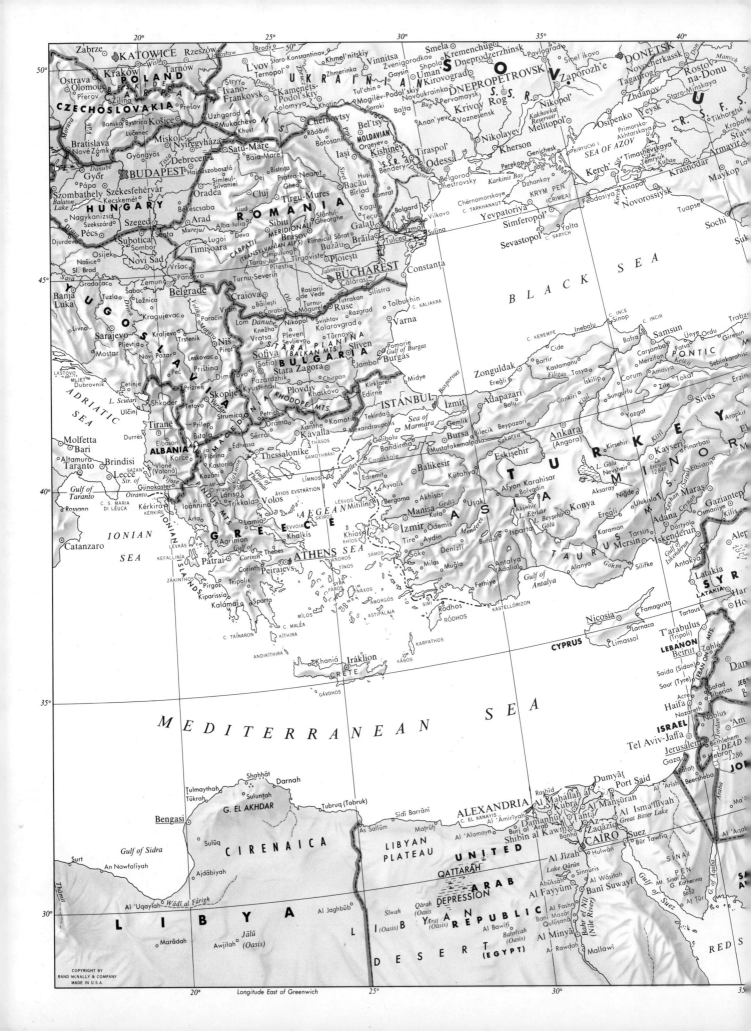